Real Feature Writing

~≈~

WITHDRAWN

LEA'S COMMUNICATION SERIES

Jennings Bryant/Dolf Zillmann, General Editors

Selected titles in Journalism (Maxwell McCombs, Advisory Editor)

DeFleur • Computer-Assisted Investigative Reporting

Fensch • Sports Writing Handbook, Second Edition

Garrison • Computer-Assisted Reporting, Second Edition

Garrison • Successful Strategies for Computer-Assisted Reporting

Hachten • The Troubles of Journalism: A Critical Look at What's Right and Wrong With the Press

Merritt • Public Journalism and Public Life: Why Telling the News is Not Enough, Second Edition

Parsigian • Mass Media Writing

Titchener • Reviewing the Arts, Second Edition

Weaver/Wilhoit • The American Journalist in the 1990s: U.S. News People at the End of an Era

For a complete list of other titles in LEA's Communication Series, please contact Lawrence Erlbaum Associates, Publishers.

Real Feature Writing

~≈~

Abraham Aamidor
The Indianapolis Star

LEA LAWRENCE ERLBAUM ASSOCIATES, PUBLISHERS
1999   Mahwah, New Jersey   London

Copyright © 1999 by Lawrence Erlbaum Associates, Inc.
All rights reserved. No part of this book may be reproduced in
any form, by photostat, microfilm, retrieval system, or any other
means, without prior written permission of the publisher.

Lawrence Erlbaum Associates, Inc., Publishers
10 Industrial Avenue
Mahwah, NJ 07430

Cover design by Kathryn Houghtaling Lacey

Library of Congress Cataloging-in-Publication Data

Aamidor, Abraham.
Real feature writing / by Abraham Aamidor.

p.   cm.

Includes bibliographical references and indexes.
ISBN 0-8058-3179-7 (cloth : alk. paper) —ISBN 0-8058-3180-0
(pbk. : alk. paper).
1. Feature writing. I. Title.
PN4784.F37A18   1999
070.4'4—dc21   98-45245
                                                              CIP

Books published by Lawrence Erlbaum Associates are printed on
acid-free paper, and their bindings are chosen for strength and du-
rability.

Printed in the United States of America
10 9 8 7 6 5 4 3 2 1

Contents

Introduction

I wanted to call this book *Everything I Ever Really Needed to Know I Learned on the Features Desk,* but that title, or one pretty close to it, already was taken. Something about learning the lessons of life in kindergarten.

Nevertheless, such a claim would be quite valid. As a veteran newspaper feature writer with 14 years of experience in Indianapolis, St. Louis, and Champaign, Illinois, I was privileged to meet, and learn from:

- A young college student born with deadly cystic fibrosis who became a child chess prodigy, then a martial arts expert and vigorous campaigner for the rights of the disabled.
- A woman from the "hollows" of West Virginia who went on to earn her doctorate at Purdue University and later write a successful magazine advice column.
- And, a beautiful dance instructor who taught me to do the lambada, billed as the world's sexiest dance at the time.

Are you a baseball fan? I remember interviewing Tommy John from his boyhood home in Terre Haute, Indiana. The left-handed pitcher won 288 games in a wonderful baseball career that spanned 3 decades, mostly with the White Sox, Yankees, and Dodgers. Sports writers often referred to him as "the man with the bionic arm" because he had so many surgeries on his pitching arm during his long career.

Tommy John had a reputation for being a fierce competitor, a man on a mission, but also for being a truly nice guy. He was all these things, and more. For Tommy John was nobody's fool.

"You know how when you get knocked out of the box early in a game, everybody will pat you on the behind and say, 'Tough luck, Tommy,' or 'You'll get 'em next time, Tommy,'" he told me during an interview. "But what they're really thinking is, 'I'm glad you got hit hard, Tommy,' and 'I hope you lose every start for the rest of the year, Tommy,' because what they really want is your spot in the starting rotation. The worse you do the better it is for them."

I learned from Tommy John, too. I told myself on the way back to the office after this particular interview that I better not turn in a weak story. There would always be younger, more ambitious writers waiting for me to fail just so they could take my spot on the features rotation.

Features has been defined as news you don't need to know, but you want to know. This may surprise you, but I disagree with such a definition. Features is the news below the surface; features is the shadow truths we don't always recognize, but that affect us all the same; features is the mysterious world on the other side of the mountain and all the amazing people and places and things that we do need to know about, even if we don't know it yet.

In addition to working for several newspapers during my career, I also have taught feature writing at Indiana University in Bloomington and at Georgia Southern University in Statesboro. I've forced students to read thick, even arcane, textbooks with more do's and don'ts and rules of the road than found in one of those driving manuals you had to memorize when you were 16. And I've used highly annotated collections that were geared more for the professional journalist than the cub reporter. I've even employed books that promised to make the reader a successful magazine writer, book author, section editor, feature writer, and beat reporter *all in one!* They're like those vitamin supplements you can buy at the mall: Take these pills and you'll shed weight, improve your memory, and have a great sex life *all in one!*

Real Feature Writing follows the "less is more" philosophy common to the best writing books. I do not try to teach you everything about writing. I don't know everything about writing, if truth be told. Nor do I claim that my book answers every possible question you might ever have about feature writing—hey, it doesn't!

Here's the "less is more" philosophy in a nutshell. Imagine you want to be a top pro tennis player—the next Steffi Graf or Pete Sampras. You'll need lots of dedication and hard work and practice and challenging matches (like tackling difficult story assignments). Yet, ultimately, you need only master a few basic facets of the game—a strong forehand, an accurate backhand, and a powerful serve. Master just those three parts of the game and you will win the Davis Cup every time.

So it is with story types and feature writing. Master my easy-to-follow techniques and you'll be a starter, if not a star, on almost any paper you can name.

This book focuses on what I believe are the most common types of feature stories in major metropolitan U.S. newspapers.

We'll look at the *profile*—of a person, place, thing, or historical event—first. You may already have written a simple personality profile or two as part of an introductory newswriting class, but this book goes beyond the very basic type of story. For example, almost anyone could do an interesting profile of pop singer and actress Madonna (if she would agree to be interviewed, of course). But did you realize you could do a profile of a coal mining disaster that killed dozens, and write that story years after the mine was closed? I did precisely this when I found the sole survivor of a terrible mine cave-in in Sullivan, IN. My primary source was now very aged and still shackled by the terrible memories of it all; another source was a younger man who made it his life's work to preserve all details and records of the calamitous event for future generations.

Then we'll examine the *trend story*. At its simplest a trend story refers to something new or emerging in society (such as the rise of the two-income family or the appearance of grunge on the music scene). It could also present a downward trend (say, the paucity of home visits by doctors or the disappearance of grunge music). Many business stories are trend stories: Unemployment is up, and inflation is down. But I've done successful, fun trend stories on the popularity of Super Soaker water guns as well as Tear Jerkers sour gum. (I personally prefer Tear Jerkers to Cry Babies, but most adults can't stand either.) In this book you'll read about trends in the teaching profession as well as an oddball trend in mail-order brides in the late 1990s.

Next, we'll look at the *"pro and con" story*. There are two sides to every story, or so the saying goes. Perhaps the most honorable tradition in journalism is that of giving both sides of a story; this is what people refer to when they say they want fair and unbiased coverage. Plus, pro and con stories can make for feisty reading, and they're often surprisingly easy to report.

There also is a chapter dealing with the *news peg*. Lots of features are generated by smaller news stories you see every day in the press. I remember a story in *The Savannah Morning News* in early 1997 about an escort service employee (read: prostitute) who was murdered in an area motel. It was your typical, sleazy detective magazine crime, until the reader discovered the victim was a housewife, complete with kids, suburban home, and minivan. She worked part-time as a prostitute. The Savannah paper followed up this news story with solid coverage—a story on the suspect, who was apprehended in Florida; a story on the extradition proceedings; a story on his arraignment; and more. In general, good crime reporting mirrors the criminal justice system: Each new development, such as jury selection, or the verdict and sentencing at the end of the trial (if the suspect is convicted) leads to a new story.

But the newspaper also did a backgrounder on several escort services operating in Savannah. It was eye-opening to see how brazen these businesses could be and how little local police and prosecutors seemed to care. The murder was the news peg.

Anniversary stories are always a variation of the news peg. Let's say you're doing a story on the anniversary of the bombing of Pearl Harbor, which marked the United States' entry into World War II, the deadliest war in history to date. You might find an aged Navy veteran who was there, in Hawaii, on December 7, 1941, during the attack. (Or, you might find the son or grandson of a Japanese pilot who helped in the attack; perhaps he's working at a local, Japanese-owned factory in your town.) You'll read a story about baseball legends Jackie Robinson and Pee Wee Reese later in this book; the story was occasioned by the 50th anniversary of Robinson's appearance in the Major Leagues, but is included here as a profile story.

We'll also look at the *focus story*. Several other books use the concept of a focus story, also known as the *microcosm/macrocosm model*, and they're right to do it. Imagine you're writing about the Red River and the destruction in Grand Forks, North Dakota, during the great flood of 1997. You can focus on one family's trials and tribulations and their efforts to rebuild after the water receded as a way of illustrating what happened to all the families affected by that natural catastrophe. A focus story helps you avoid getting stuck in the mud of too many facts, too many statistics, too many names of too many people that readers just can't follow.

I often think in terms of *problems and solutions*, as in the question, "What's the problem here, and what are people doing to solve it?" If you, as reporter, can identify the central problem affecting the people you're writing about, then you are well on your way to writing the entire story. Say, for example, that the local municipality has a lot of garbage on its hands (*the problem*) and wants to build a new garbage incinerator (*the solution*) near a poor neighborhood in the older, industrial part of town. Yet this solution may in turn lower property values and the quality of life in those neighborhoods affected by the proposed solution (call this the law of unintended consequences).

The lead for this story could simply be a report that the municipality has announced the new incinerator and has explained why it's so beneficial. But your story will take off from that point: You might focus on the health hazards, if any, the incinerator poses. Or, you could feature a community activist who singlehandedly is seeking to block the hated incinerator. In fact, you could do all these things, and more. Write about the high-handed way in which government sometimes makes its decisions, or write about the history we have in this country of victimizing poorer people by dumping unwanted projects in their backyards, not ours.

Maybe you'll include a section on the neighborhood that once was, depending on how "feature-y" you want to get and whether your editors will support you.

Ultimately you must write about the reaction within the community to the challenge the incinerator poses. Perhaps there will be a compromise hammered out by community activists and city leaders. The possibilities for reporting and the issues you need to address in your story become apparent once you've identified the central problem and the people who are fighting for solutions.

There's another, simpler way to address the question of "problems and solutions," however. Simply ask yourself the following question: Who was affected by the news, and what did they do about it?

The *journalistic essay* is a form of *explanatory writing*. Such essays can be wordy and look a lot like long editorials, but when they are done well, the writer will assume an authoritative voice, get his or her facts together and quote appropriate sources, and will really seek to explain the news, not just report it. This can be as simple as explaining "why" so many people felt close to Princess Diana of England when she died in 1997, "how" the United States misread the events that preceded the fall of the Shah of Iran in 1979, or "what" is behind the push for reparations for slavery in parts of the African American community. Journalistic essays do not necessarily lead to *advocacy journalism*, however. Sometimes the essayist is merely trying to present the "other side of the story" or include facts left out of daily news reports (an example of this might be trying to explain the factors behind, say, rioting and revolution in a Third World country).

In the final chapter of Part II we'll look at *point of view* more closely than you did in your basic news reporting and writing classes. In literature, point of view usually refers to the point of view of the narrator. Most of you have read Harper Lee's *To Kill A Mockingbird*, about a little girl growing up in the South and her father's defense of a Black man charged with a terrible crime. Most commentators feel that story was told from the point of view of the little girl, although obviously an adult wrote the book.

It's worth keeping this notion of point of view in mind when you hunt a good feature story: Maybe you'll tell a cancer story from the point of view of the doctor, the patient, or the spouse of the patient. Maybe you'll do a war story from the point of view of a general, a foot soldier, or a refugee family.

For purposes of this book, point of view also includes taking a stand on an issue, even taking sides. Perhaps you were taught to be completely objective in your writing; to be neutral, dispassionate, impartial; not to adopt one point of view over another. In fact, this book is going to put you on a longer leash than you've ever been allowed before when it comes to violating notions of impartiality or neutral points of view.

But let me first defend the notion of "objectivity" from its many cynical critics on campus and in the media today. Objectivity is an ideal: The closer we come to it, the better off we are. Objectivity provides a standard by which we can rate our journalistic efforts, and it gives our many critics a legitimate stick with which to beat us when we fall short of our stated goal of objectivity.

Nevertheless, there are times when a writer—and not just an editorial writer—will adopt a certain point of view in a story or seek to change the reader's mind about an important issue of the day. Imagine you've been sent by the Associated Press to report on the genocide in Rwanda; imagine you were sent to cover the Communist atrocities against more than a million Cambodians in the late 1970s; imagine you were a witness to the Nazi Holocaust against the Jews during World War II. Frankly, you would be expected to report on how evil these things were, and how these evil things were being perpetrated, for the express purpose of mobilizing sentiment against such horrible practices. Any neutrality, or lack of empathy for these and myriad other victims in the world, would be hard to fathom.

There also are several chapters in the last part of the book that deal with such traditional feature writing topics as writing the lead, observation for detail, interview techniques, use of quotes, online databases, and more. But you'll find that all these topics are actually dealt with in the chapters on story type and structure. Real writers start with the nub or concept of a story, then expand this. It is a mistake to assume that good writers piece together a story like a quilt from separate, distinct parts called quotes or adverbs or summaries; books that emphasize the parts more than the whole are misleading.

Of course you should worry about engaging leads, crisp sentences, and keen visual observations in your writing, but all this is what Pulitzer Prize-winning journalist and teacher Jon Franklin calls "the polish stage" of writing, as in applying the polish to a solidly built piece of furniture (Franklin, 1994, pp. 11, 44). If you haven't told a good story to begin with, and your reporting has more holes in it than Swiss cheese, no amount of polish will make it good.

This book is organized along proven lines. In each chapter of the first two sections you'll find an introduction to the topic, including advice on structuring and outlining your own stories. This book is BIG on structure. (You wouldn't build a house without putting up a frame first, would you? So why would you write a story without having a solid structure or frame to pin everything on?)

The introduction in all cases is followed by one or two real newspaper feature stories that illustrate the point of the chapter. Next you'll find a detailed analysis of the story or stories you've just read. This latter section is important because it's where we put the story under the microscope. We'll analyze why certain things were included in the story and perhaps question what could have been added or omitted as well.

Each chapter closes with a suggested writing assignment or two, including useful tips on how to complete the assignment.

Good writing is emphasized throughout the book. But what if you're not a "gifted" writer? What if you want to be a feature writer because you like the variety of topics and challenges you'll encounter, and not because you're in love with what has been called "the writer's life"?

No prob-lem-o! I have spoken with successful editors, writing coaches, and journalism teachers around the country, and every one of them puts reporting and structure ahead of pure writing skill in terms of what makes a winning story.

Or, as one teacher at Southern Illinois University-Carbondale said to me, "Good thinking is good writing."

Some of the stories featured in the following chapters are mine; most come from other writers. I've included some of mine because I believe them to be good stories, but also because I know what I was thinking when I wrote them: You'll get more out of the analyses.

I've selected stories from other sources when I think they illustrate the chapter topics well. In part, you can consider this book to be a "reader," that is, a collection of worthwhile stories to read, even if it's just when you're on that long plane ride over Thanksgiving break, or if you have a few free hours in the evening.

Many of the stories included in this book have been read at one time or another by students in my classes in Bloomington, IN, and Statesboro, GA. These stories passed the most difficult test of all in that they actually held the interest of students just like yourself!

So, whether you're using this book as required reading for a college class, or you're a beat reporter on a small daily trying to move up, or even if you're a lay person who just wants to understand what constitutes a good newspaper feature story, get ready for a nice ride across the lives and times of some wonderful and strange and astonishing people and events in the contemporary United States.

Real Feature Writing
Part I

1

The Profile

Did you ever meet a celebrity? Cindy Crawford, perhaps? Or, The Reverend Jesse Jackson, or Chipper Jones or Michelle Kwan or Mel Gibson or Hillary Rodham Clinton?

What's the first question a friend would ask you if you had met any of the above celebrities?

I guarantee you it would be, "What's he or she like?"

This is inevitable. Magazines like *People, TV Digest,* and *Rolling Stone,* and newspaper feature sections from Portland, Maine, to Portland, Oregon, are filled with stories every day that basically answer the question, "What's he or she like?"

Martha Stewart is famous for her home decorating and gardening tips, as well as her own magazine and successful line of products at a major department store chain. But some stories I've seen on Martha Stewart call her a controlling person who can be hard to get along with. That's what she's like.

The late baseball player Jackie Robinson was the first African American to break the color line in the major leagues. He was chosen for the task at hand by executives of the Brooklyn Dodgers because he was a gentleman who made as good an impression off the field as on. But he was also a fierce competitor who resented that some people might think he was a lackey, or what used to be called a "plantation Black."That's what he was like.

And it's not just personalities we're talking about. Think of the last travel story you read, perhaps as part of your research into vacation destinations for yourself. Did you ever want to travel to London? Timbuktu, perhaps? Before you would commit to any place, though, you'd have to know what to expect, or—what it's like!

You could say the same for an automobile review, which is a kind of profile, too. Hey, man, what's it like to drive a Dodge Viper at more than 140 miles per hour?

Imagine you've interviewed someone who spent the last 2 years in a biodome, hermetically sealed off from the rest of the world and confined to a small space with just a few other people. You would have to ask the person, "What was it like?"

Sometimes what you find may not be very agreeable, of course. Too often profiles really are nothing but "puff pieces," little more than public relations jobs meant to enhance the image of the profile subject. That may not be surprising, because people with something to hide typically won't agree to a profile in the first place.

I wrote a profile several years ago of Jack Crawford, the first director of the Indiana lottery. Jack was a Notre Dame graduate—first in his class, as I recall—and was a top prosecutor in Lake County, that crime-riddled part of northeast Indiana that borders Chicago. Jack was a young, handsome, highly competent, and ambitious politico whose future in Indiana politics seemed assured.

But he was brought down by a sex scandal while in office and he resigned in disgrace. Many reporters in Indiana recall the press conference in which Crawford bowed his head and began sobbing uncontrollably, then announced his resignation.

I wrote about Jack after the fall. I had a better-than-average profile going in because there had been some real news here. This wasn't just another pretty face after all. Plus, there was the titillation factor. People would read about this guy if for no other reason than the humiliating nature of his particular sex scandal.

Jack didn't have to speak to me. But there wasn't much more he could hide from the public, either, so he agreed. His wife had left him; he was driving a second-hand Chevrolet Cavalier because he was broke; and he shared office space with another attorney in a small shopping center up around 62nd and Keystone Streets in Indianapolis, most definitely not a place where the rich and powerful gathered. Talk about how the mighty had fallen!

This man was down, but he was not out. My story turned out to be a profile of the indomitable human spirit. Jack held his head high and was determined to rebuild his career—and his name—as best he could. He was doing criminal defense work at the time I met him, which was ironic because he had been one of the state's toughest and most successful prosecutors in his heyday. I spent some time with Jack in court and followed his style closely: He was a great defense attorney. I remember telling friends this was the guy I'd hire if I ever got in trouble with the law. Naturally, he knew all the tricks and weaknesses of the lesser prosecutors he confronted daily.

I tried to speak with Jack's former wife and some of his former associates as well. The wife said no, and some of his old friends turned out to be proverbial fair weather friends. That was all part of the tragedy and part of the story I reported.

But I guarantee you this: My profile was no puff piece. It had some real grit and substance to it. And it proved there is indeed life after death, in a manner of speaking.

The basic strategy in reporting and writing a profile is to spend time with the subject. As much as possible. Do not do a phone interview and expect to know what a person is like. If it's a personality profile of, say, the first woman mayor in your town, visit her at her office, sure. But also visit her at her home, with her husband and children (if applicable), or perhaps at her favorite retreat.

Maybe she likes to sing in the church choir, or perhaps she's on a bowling team. Then by all means visit with her at these venues, too, and talk to people who know about this other side in her life.

As part of your background research, you'd read other stories that may have been written about her, or you'd look for her name in any previous stories about local government and development issues. You'd also look at applicable campaign financial statements and talk to people who worked with her in the past, but who have no stake in her career at present. (This latter point is important because former associates may speak more candidly than current associates.)

And when your research and interviewing are over, tell the reader "the facts," but also tell about the Mayor's smile and moods, her passions and peeves, and the way she likes to dress and act when she's out of the limelight; tell the reader what she's like in her most private moments as well as when she's on center stage. Tell the reader enough so that he or she can decide what the mayor is really like.

The following story is a profile of a … trailer park. First, you have my permission to laugh and giggle, and chortle and snicker and do whatever it is you have to do. But leave all your preconceptions and stereotypes of life in a trailer park at the door.

"*My Gawd*, he's writin' about a dang *trailer park!*"

Finished laughing? OK. Now, let me tell you, first and foremost, that it is real people who live in trailer parks. That was the one unalterable truth I carried with me, along with my pen and reporter's notebook, when I went looking for this story, which overtly is a profile.

Who are these people who live in trailers? What's it like to live in a trailer?

And, why? Why would anyone live in a trailer in the first place?

This should sound like I was working off the time-honored "inverted pyramid," that reporting and writing model which always calls for answering the 5 W's and H. If truth be told, every story must answer the 5 W's and H (who, what, when, where, why, and how) at some point, although not necessarily at the top of the story.

The story you're about to read is set in Johnson County, Indiana, just south of Indianapolis. Indiana has one of the highest concentrations of trailer park housing in the country, and the state is a leading manufacturer of mobile homes and trailers, so it was a good story to do for *The Indianapolis Star*. We had featured life in small towns, hippy communes, religious communities, inner-city neighborhoods, trendy downtown redevelopments, and more, but amazingly, had almost completely ignored people who lived in trailer parks (except for the occasional tornado or fire story, of course).

Because there were so many trailer parks in Central Indiana—my newspaper's circulation area—I felt it was impossible to report on all of them, or even very many, in an adequate way. I would have to *focus* on one community. (Note that you're going to see a later chapter devoted to focus stories, but none of these distinctions or story types are mutually exclusive. A story can be a profile, and a focus story, and an expanded inverted pyramid, all at the same time. The ultimate question will be, "Was it a good story?")

Consequently, I went stalking the perfect trailer park. I literally visited five or six different communities and made observations and took notes, before I even committed to writing a story. I ultimately chose a place called Friendly Village because it was neither the poorest nor the most splendiferous; it was neither the largest nor the smallest, but it was representative of many parks. (Plus, I really loved the name.) It was quite photogenic, too: Friendly Village has a nice swimming pool and large, welcoming gate in front, just like a vacation or campsite, as well as its own small fishing hole and other little touches. This was important because I knew ahead of time that we'd run a bunch of color photos with the story.

There was another factor. I spoke to management at Friendly Village and they seemed very cooperative; they had no objections to me and a photographer coming on to their property and interviewing folks. Friendly Village is on private property and trespassing was an issue.

Go ahead and read the story now.

                                                 ≈

Upward Mobility*
by Abe Aamidor

Harry Wagner was mad; he wasn't going to take it anymore.

A longtime resident of the Friendly Village trailer park in northwestern Johnson County, he had seen enough break-ins, street-corner fights and speeding cars to be disgusted with it all. In 1984 he banded together with other residents of the sprawling, 500-unit mobile home

---

*From "Upward Mobility" by A. Aamidor. Copyright © 1995, *The Indianapolis Star*. Reprinted by permission.

community and formed one of the very first Crime Watch programs in a trailer park in the country.

"We never went in to get someone ourselves, but there'd be 15 or 20 of us standing around a trailer until the police showed up," the 50-year-old commercial refrigeration technician said almost gleefully.

"Would *you* want to come out and face all those angry people if you were a burglar?"

Imagine those Friendly Village residents—retirees and late-shift workers who needed their sleep, and countless single mothers—with their citizens band radios in hand, all ready to bolt from their long, narrow steel homes the instant their scanners alerted them to a robbery in progress.

And it worked. Crime dropped and remains down in Friendly Village, which then was Shady Brook Heights, according to Maj. Steve Byerly of the Johnson County Sheriff's Department, who helped Wagner start the program.

The 1,600 people who live in Friendly Village are part of a nation within a nation that's tucked away at the edges of the American Dream, out of sight of the mainstream and out of the news except for an occasional scare story during tornado season. They are people often plagued by stereotypes.

About 10 million Americans live in 4 million manufactured homes in 25,000 communities, according to the Manufactured Housing Institute in Arlington, Va. In Indiana an estimated 460,000 people reside in all types of manufactured homes, including what are traditionally called trailers. That's nearly 10 percent of the state's population.

"Not everybody can live in $200,000 homes in Carmel," said Thomas Corson, chairman of Coachman Industries in Elkhart, until recently a major manufacturer of mobile homes. "It's an important segment of housing."

Paradise Lost and Found

Harry Wagner, a heavy-set, Buddha-like presence known throughout Friendly Village for his mutton-chop sideburns and the radio-controlled car club he helps run, has built a private Eden on his small lot. He and his wife Barbara have a flower garden alongside the metal skirt of their trailer, a cozy wood deck by their front door and a small picnic table in the shade of the poplar and dogwood trees in their front yard.

Nearby, in one of the other looping courts within the 68-acre park, Billy Parker is bent over an old Chrysler he bought for $80, troubleshooting some engine problems under the hood.

Parker recently bought his "fixer-upper" trailer for $1,000. It definitely was not in move-in condition, but it's a start, says the 29-year-old concrete mixer truck driver.

A divorced father of two, Parker lives in the trailer alone except on the weekends when he cares for his daughters, ages 3 and 5. In the five months he's been in his home, he has replaced some of the water pipes, repaired the roof and fixed seams in the sheet metal exterior walls that literally were coming apart. But it's home to him.

"Oh, yeah, it was definitely the money," said Parker, explaining why he chose to live in a trailer.

"I could spend $400 to $500 (a month) on an apartment, plus the utilities, or I could move in here for a lot less money, and I've got three bedrooms for my girls."

Like the other residents in Friendly Village, Parker must abide by several management-imposed "stipulations." They include no privacy fence; no wading pool for the kids (this one is widely ignored); no satellite TV dishes (you must buy your cable TV service from the park management); and no major auto repairs on the street, such as "dropping" a transmission or overhauling an engine (this one also is ignored on occasion).

Still, Parker figures he is saving money compared to renting an apartment elsewhere in Johnson County, where he grew up. Besides, there *is* a countrylike charm to the narrow, winding lanes that branch out everywhere in Friendly Village, and to the little, unnamed creek that flows just behind the park.

Other amenities include a convenience store that operates outside the main entrance and small swimming pool on the grounds that is open in warm weather. A meeting room is available to residents in the main office building, and the management even tosses seasonal parties for the residents, including an annual summer cookout and a community-wide garage sale.

Compared to traditional single-family homes built on a foundation, trailers, mobile homes or manufactured housing—all three terms are used—are considered questionable investments by some. Larger, top-of-the-line mobile homes can cost as much as $35,000 set up and skirted; barely adequate used homes in the area cost $3,500 and up, though "fixer-uppers" are cheaper.

Many banks will make loans on mobile homes, but they are financed like cars. When the home is paid off, you get a title, not a deed.

Worse, mobile homes depreciate in value, just like a car.

But worst of all, to some people's thinking, is the "lot rent" you must pay for the privilege of setting your trailer down in someone else's trailer court. Lot rental at Friendly Village, for example, is $213 a month.

No matter. For many mobile home owners, the purchase price represents not so much an investment as a stepping stone to true home ownership.

As the World Turns

By the front entrance, on County Line Road, a large painted sign beckons passers-by, as if the trailer park is a campground or tourist attraction. Bertha Upton, whose trailer is near the front, says she has the best seat in the house for the parade of humanity that passes her rectangular steel home every day. She's lived at Friendly Village for 12 years.

Upton is retired, but every day she says she watches the yellow school buses pick up the children who assemble at the stop near her home; and in the afternoons she waves to her neighbors who pull up to the mailboxes, which are almost at her doorstep.

"I started (living in trailers) when my child's daughter was born," recalled Upton, 70, who still drives a full-size pickup truck she parks on a concrete slab beside her trailer.

"I had six rooms of furniture and she lived in a trailer, and she said, 'Mom, I don't want to bring up my children in a trailer,' so I traded her the six rooms of furniture for her trailer. I was renting an apartment at the time."

Now, Upton's children and grown grandchildren regularly come by to mow the grass or resurface the trailer roof. The latter is a particularly thankless but necessary chore for all trailer owners. It involves spreading a thick, watertight goop across the entire top with a heavy brush, preferably when the weather is as hot as can be so the stuff will seal better.

At the other end of Friendly Village's generational spectrum are kids. Lots of kids. The park's narrow streets are so packed with schoolchildren in the afternoon that, for safety reasons, the buses won't go inside to drop off their charges. Instead, they are let out at the entrance.

Nearly 200 children from Friendly Village and two smaller mobile home communities attend Pleasant Grove Elementary School in Johnson County. That's about a fourth of the school's enrollment of 742.

Principal Roger Micnerski typically greets his schoolchildren as they amble in to classes every morning. Standing just inside the front doors, thrown wide for another morning's arrivals, Micnerski challenged a visitor to tell which children were from the trailer parks and which from the pricey new homes so prominent in booming White River Township, one of the fastest-growing areas in central Indiana.

It wasn't easy: Virtually all the children were white, and printed T-shirts and name-brand athletic shoes look pretty much the same on all kids.

Yet some children went one way—into the nearby cafeteria for their breakfasts, where those who receive free and reduced-price meals always go—while the others went straight down the antiseptic hallways to their classrooms.

Almost without exception, the children clamoring for food every morning are from the trailer parks. According to Micnerski, 134 children receive free meals, and 20 get reduced-price meals at the school.

Micnerski said staff do not discriminate against the less-well-to-do. About 75 percent of his teachers already have signed up for a special program to begin in the spring that will focus on bringing out the best in all children. Still, many of the poorer parents are defensive about their social status, he says.

"'Are you going to look at me as an equal? Are you going to work with me?' they'll ask," Micnerski said. "That's one of our jobs, to break down that defensiveness."

Home school adviser Patti Duckworth says one of the problems families from the trailer parks have to endure is the attitude of others.

"I've had parents sitting around the Little League games and they'll say, 'Oh, I hear they're starting another program for *those* kids,'" she said.

Some of the trailer park children have been and are in the school's gifted-and-talented program. But the numbers are disproportionately small.

At the high school level, it is hard to discern graduation and high school drop-out rates. Center Grove High School does not keep statistics by residency.

Brandon Fox, 21, a longtime Friendly Village resident, dropped out of Center Grove High School and says he completed his education at Emmerich Manual High School in Indianapolis. He hates Center Grove High.

"The school gave us a bad reputation," claimed Fox, who's lived at Friendly Village for 17 years and frequently has been unemployed.

"They don't like us because we're low-income."

His evidence? "All my friends that were from the trailer park, if they missed school for even a day, (the school) would make the call," Fox said. "But if you weren't from the trailer park, they wouldn't call on you."

A teen-ager who is still in high school says there is no problem with teachers or administration. But there *is* a social stigma attached to being from the "trailer park," she claims. Jennifer Frambes is a 16-year-old sophomore at Center Grove High.

"Some people don't talk to people from here," Frambes said. "They have more money than us."

Close Quarter

Whatever the case, life goes on in Friendly Village.

Neighbors talk about recent mobile home sale prices like stock brokers watch Wall Street quotations: they cast fishing lines from the small bridge over the creek and hope to get lucky; they bounce basketballs along the blacktop on weekends, looking for a pick-up game; they stop by Harry Wagner's place to look at his RC car collection.

Tim Mason, 34, has lived at the park for nearly two years. He lives with his 3-year-old son, David, girlfriend Cindy King and her two children in an older trailer he bought for $3,500.

Currently unemployed, Mason has been building a large deck in front of his trailer from scrap wood he's found at nearby construction sites. The deck will feature a long ramp for his wheelchair-bound son, a stroke victim who has cerebral palsy.

Mason likes it at Friendly Village. He's been to the creek many times with neighborhood children, who helped him build a rock garden at one end of his trailer, and some of the older park teens—even the ones who look rough, he says—stop by to poke and tickle his son, which the boy loves.

Mason and his girlfriend live in Friendly Village because it's the cheapest option available.

"I feel there's a comfortable atmosphere here," Mason said. "They're not all new trailers here. They're not all run-down, either."

"The people here are all easy to get along with, too. I guess they're all common people."

~·~·~

I say that this story is a profile of a place (maybe of a lifestyle, perhaps of a situation that the residents found themselves in). But trailers don't talk, and although leaves on trees may whisper in the breeze, they don't talk, either. At least, not literally. When you are doing a profile of a place or a thing, you still must interview people—the people who are associated with the place or thing.

There's another source of information for such profiles (and any other story where you're doing firsthand reporting). I'm reminded of the old story in the Bible of the patriarch Abraham (or prophet Ibrihim, as he would be known in Islam). Abraham complained that the idols of his day had eyes, but did not see, and ears, but did not hear.

That's right: Idols don't really use their eyes and ears and other senses, but you do. You are an observer; one of your key reporting tools is *observation*. You are the eyes and ears of the reader; you are the reader's agent and advocate; you are getting the story on behalf of your reader, who unfortunately could not be on assignment with you.

So include little swatches and tidbits of what you saw and heard and felt and observed during your visit or visits to the site of your story, even if some of these observations go beyond "facts" or "quotes."

The thick goop being spread on the trailer roof tops, the school buses trundling up to the front gates in the afternoon, and kids looking for a basketball game or fishing in the little creek that runs through the park: Include it all. I would say you could even include more physical description than I did here, but this is somewhat arguable: Note that the original story included many photographs of people quoted, and some editors and reporters feel it is redundant to include too much physical description in the text.

Note how I began the story by writing about a man named Harry Wagner. For all you know, I could be writing a profile of Harry, except that it quickly becomes clear that Harry is one of the folks who makes Friendly Village a real place. I have employed an *anecdotal lead*, a little story at the beginning that is emblematic of what is yet to come. Telling about residents banding together to fight crime also makes the park a real place.

I also provide plenty of facts and figures in this story—how many trailers, how many residents, how much money, and so on. I believe the reader needs to know that a whopping 10 million Americans live in trailers, and that 10% of Indiana residents do. A profile cannot be entirely impressionistic.

Identifying *expert sources* of information for this story was fairly straightforward, too. I looked in the *Encyclopedia of Associations*, available in almost all libraries and through some online computer services as well. I checked that encyclopedia's keyword index, using terms like "mobile home," "trailer," and the like to identify suitable sources. The *Encyclopedia of Associations* is one of the greatest sources of information on nearly 10,000 different activities, associations, and special interest groups; listings almost always include a contact person and phone number. People and organizations that list in the *Encyclopedia of Associations* are almost always eager to talk to people doing stories, including students doing papers and articles for class.

So, I dutifully included facts and figures in my profile of a trailer park. But mostly I stuck with real people interviews. Grandmotherly Bertha Upton traded furniture for her daughter's trailer: Bertha didn't need a big place and her daughter wanted to move into a real house one day. Single dad Billy Parker didn't have much money, so he bought a thoroughly trashed trailer for $1,000 and fixed it up himself. It's home to him and his two children.

I'm clearly sympathetic to the modest lives these trailer park residents lead, but I don't cover up the problems, either. I included the teenage angst of one young high school dropout who says teachers at the local high school don't like kids from the trailer park. Of course, the school officials get a chance to express their point of view that the poor are defensive about their situation.

The story is not perfect. I'm now convinced that I put too many numbers and figures too high up in the story, for one thing. You'll see a story from a *Miami Herald* reporter later in this book that deals with the health insurance crisis in the United States. He includes three times as many numbers in his story as I did in mine, but he handles them better, parceling out the data throughout the story, and always in the context of supporting some greater point he wants to make. Look for "Stayin' Alive" by John Dorschner in chapter 5.

Still, I like the story about Friendly Village. I liked most of the people I met; more than that, I learned to respect many of them. I could imagine myself growing up in such a place (I lived in rental apartments growing up in Chicago).

Several weeks after the story ran I was driving by County Line Road, which separates Johnson County from Indianapolis' Marion County, and I decided to pull in to Friendly Village for a follow-up visit. I saw Tim Mason playing with his disabled son in the late afternoon sun. Tim was the unemployed man who built a ramp for the wheelchair-bound boy out of scrap wood he found at a nearby construction site.

"I didn't know if I really wanted to talk to you or not," Tim told me during that follow-up visit. "I didn't know if you were going to make us look bad or not. But I was real pleased with how the story came out."

In some stories, with some sources, I guess we reporters "make people look bad." It's what the public thinks, anyway. But in this story, at least, I think I got it just right.

Without a doubt the first feature story you ever wrote was a personality profile. That's why this book begins with the profile. Such stories can be easy to do, and if the person has had an interesting life, or currently has an interesting job or lifestyle, people will read the story.

The next story you're about to analyze is, on the face of it, a profile of baseball legend Jackie Robinson. No matter that he's dead: Biographical texts typically are written about dead people! There are plenty of sources around who would remember Robinson, and there are plenty of published quotes and facts from his life you could use in your story, as long as you give proper attribution and don't lift too much from other published sources.

But as you read "At Robinson's Side, Reese helped change baseball" you'll see the story is also about shortstop Pee Wee Reese, the captain of the Brooklyn Dodgers who had to overcome his own prejudices to help integrate his baseball team.

And the most perceptive among you conclude that this a profile of neither Robinson nor Reese, but really a quite simple and honest story whose only mission is to tell us the way it was all those years ago.

~~~~

At Robinson's Side: Reese helped change baseball*
by Ira Berkow

The white boy was 13 or 14, and his brother was about 16, when, with dusk descending on that summer day in Louisville, Ky., in the early 1930s, the older boy shouted a racial slur at six black kids, telling them, "Get off this street!" With that, the six black kids took chase after

*From "At Robinson's Side, Reese helped change baseball" by I. Berkouse. Copyright © 1997, The New York Times company. Reprinted by permission.

the white boys, and the two white kids ran with everything they had and made it safely home.

How did he feel about his older brother's action, the now 78-year-old man named Harold (Pee Wee) Reese was asked recently.

Reese, recuperating from surgery for lung cancer a few weeks ago, rubbed a graying eyebrow in the living room of his winter home here as he thought about the incident involving him and his brother Carl Jr.

"I thought it was stupid," he said. "I mean, to throw out a threat like that when we're six against two!"

Reese, the former star shortstop for the Brooklyn Dodgers, and a member of baseball's Hall of Fame, smiled, for of course there was much more to it than the numerical equation.

Some 15 years after that childhood incident, Pee Wee Reese became a pivotal figure in the acceptance and support of a rookie teammate, Jackie Robinson, who broke the color barrier in the major leagues in 1947.

Looking back now, 50 years after Robinson's historic breakthrough into the so-called national pastime, two moments in particular stand out between Reese and Robinson. Reese, in cream-colored short-sleeve shirt, green pants and tan buck shoes, his arms creased with age and the flesh not as tight as in his Dodger days, and a slightly tired look in his eyes from a radiation treatment in the morning, thought back upon those years.

The first of the two incidents occurred at the beginning of spring training in 1947, when Robinson had been called up to the Dodgers from Montreal, Brooklyn's top minor league team, on which Robinson had starred during the 1946 season. A petition was drawn up by a group of mostly Southern Dodgers players that stated they would not take the field with a black man.

"I'm not signing that," Reese told the ringleaders, who included Dixie Walker, Kirby Higbe and Bobby Bragan. "No way."

Reese, the soft-spoken but respected team captain, with a Southern upbringing, perhaps surprised the petition-carriers. "I wasn't thinking of myself as the Great White Father," Reese says now. "I just wanted to play baseball. I'd just come back from serving in the South Pacific with the Navy during the Second World War, and I had a wife and daughter to support. I needed the money. I just wanted to get on with it."

But there was more to it than the money.

And Reese's refusal to sign the petition, many believe, meant the end of the matter.

Robinson played, and endured vicious abuse from opposing teams, from beanballs and spikings to racial epithets and spitting. Robinson had promised Branch Rickey, the owner and general manager of the Dodgers, that for at least his first two years in the major leagues, he would hold his tongue and his fists, no matter the provocation. And one day—it was probably in Cincinnati, Reese recalled, in

1947 or 1948—the attack was so nasty that Reese walked over to Robinson and put his hand on the black man's shoulder.

"Pee Wee kind of sensed the sort of hopeless, dead feeling in me and came over and stood beside me for a while," Robinson recalled, as quoted in the forthcoming biography, *Jackie Robinson*," by Arnold Rampersad (Alfred A. Knopf). "He didn't say a word but he looked over at the chaps who were yelling at me through him and just stared. He was standing by me, I could tell you that." The hecklers ceased their attack. "I will never forget it," Robinson said.

Over the years, Reese became perhaps Robinson's best friend on the Dodgers, though there were others who were reasonably close to him as well, including the white players Carl Erskine, Gil Hodges and Ralph Branca, and, of his black teammates, Junior Gilliam in particular.

But Reese's attitude, including that defining gesture of solidarity on the field that they were, in the end, teammates and brothers under the skin, did not come from a save-the-world mentality.

"Something in my gut reacted to the moment," Reese said. "Something about—what?—the unfairness of it? The injustice of it? I don't know."

Reese's son, Mark, a 40-year-old documentary film maker, has wondered where that gut reaction from a man brought up in Southern mores came from.

"I think it might have something to do with that hanging tree in the middle of the town of Brandenburg, Ky.," Mark Reese said. Brandenburg is about 35 miles south of Louisville, and a few miles from Ekron, where the Reese family lived on a farm and where Reese's father, Carl Sr., became a railroad detective.

"When my dad was a boy of about 9 or 10 years old," Mark Reese said, "he remembers his father pointing out a tree in Brandenburg with a long branch extending out. It was there, his father told him, that black men had been lynched. I believe it was an important thing for my dad, because many times when we visited relatives in Brandenburg, he would point out that tree to me, and tell me about the lynchings. He never made a big point about the significance, but there was definitely an emotion in his voice, an emotion that said to me, anyway, that it was a terrible thing that human beings did to another human being, and only because of the color of their skin. And I imagine that when his dad told him the story, there was a similar emotion."

Still modest about his role

Pee Wee Reese shrugged his shoulders at this interpretation. It is his innate manner to play down himself, and, apparently, his contribution, particularly in the area of Jackie Robinson, where, he feels, he might only be a deflection from the limelight that Robinson deserves. In the book, "Baseball's Great Experiment," a thorough study of the black entry into baseball, the author Jules Tygiel quotes Reese telling Robinson sometime before Robinson's death at 53 in 1972, "You know I didn't go out of my way to be nice to you." And Robinson replied, "Pee Wee, maybe that's what I appreciated most."

"I seem to remember a conversation along those lines," Reese recalled in his home here. "Sounds right." He laughed.

He recalled the first time he learned about Robinson. "I was on a ship coming back to the States from Guam, in the middle of the ocean, and was playing cards. Someone hollered to me: 'Hey, Pee Wee, did you hear? The Dodgers signed a nigger.' It didn't mean that much to me and I kept playing cards. Then the guy said, 'And he plays shortstop!' My God, just my luck, Robinson has to play my position! But I had confidence in my abilities, and I thought, well, if he can beat me out, more power to him. That's exactly how I felt."

From Rivals to Partners

It turned out that Robinson, in his first year as a Dodger, would play first base, then for the next several years move to second base and team with Reese for one of the brightest double-play combinations in baseball, as the Dodgers won pennant after pennant.

Just as Reese does not give himself undue credit, he seems clear-eyed about others. And while Robinson has been raised in some circles to a near deity, Reese saw the man within.

"Jackie was a great player, a great competitor, and pretty fearless," Reese recalled. "He had only a fair arm, but made up for it at second base by never backing down when a runner came barrelling in. And he'd do some things that I wondered about. He would actually taunt some pitchers. He'd shout at them from the batter's box to just try to throw at his head! I told him: 'Jackie, quiet down. They might take you up on it. And if they're still mad, they might throw at me, too!'" Reese laughed. "And after the two years were up in which he had promised Mr. Rickey that he'd turn the other cheek, he became a guy who would stand up for himself. And he could be a tough bench jockey, and he might plow into a guy who was in his way."

One time, after Robinson had been in the league for a few years, he groused to Reese that the pitchers were throwing at him because they were racists. "No," Reese replied. "They aren't throwing at you because you're black, Jackie. They're throwing at you because they just don't like you."

Robinson smirked, and then smiled. Reese could say such things to Robinson because of their friendship, and because Robinson knew where Reese's heart—and mind—were.

After all, it was Reese who was the first Dodger in Robinson's first spring training camp to walk across the field and shake his hand. "It was the first time I'd ever shaken the hand of a black man," Reese said. "But I was the captain of the team. It was my job, I believe, to greet the new players."

But greeting, and associating with, a black man was something different, to be sure. "When I was growing up, we never played ball with blacks because they weren't allowed in the parks. And the schools were segregated, so we didn't go to school with them. And there'd be some mischief between blacks and whites, but, as I remember, it was just mischief. It wasn't hatred, at least not from me.

Challenging Bias in Small Moments

And it was Reese who first sat down in the clubhouse to play cards with Robinson. When Dixie Walker later took Reese aside and said, "How can you be playing cards with him?" Reese recalls that he replied, "Look, Dixie, you and Stell"—Walker's wife—"travel with a black woman who takes care of your kids, who cooks your food, who you trust—isn't that even more than playing cards with a black?" And Walker said, "But this is different."

But not to Reese.

Today, Reese, at 5 feet 10 inches, weighs 165 pounds, after losing nearly 15 pounds in a week's stay in the hospital after the surgery for lung cancer (he quit smoking cigarettes about 10 years ago). A third of his lung was removed. Doctors believe they have cut out the cancer, but Reese must continue to undergo radiation treatments. He is strong enough, however, to be back playing golf and on Saturday celebrated his 55th wedding anniversary with his wife, Dotty.

After his playing days, he coached with the Dodgers for one year, in 1959, then broadcast ball games for CBS and NBC and was a representative of the Louisville bat company. But for Reese, now a great-grandfather, there remain some painful physical reminders of an athletic career. He has an arthritic thumb, perhaps the result of his youth as a marbles champion, from which he derived his nickname.

And Reese walks with a slight tilt because of trouble with his knees—he has had one knee replacement and may need a second. The injuries are a result, probably, of a major league career in which he made eight All-Star teams and batted .269 over 16 seasons, 10 of those seasons with Robinson. Reese was considered one of the smartest players in the game (remember when he took the cut-off throw from Sandy Amoros and wheeled in short left field as though having eyes in the back of his head and fired the ball to first base to double off the Yankees' Gil McDougald to help preserve for Brooklyn the seventh and deciding game of the 1955 World Series?).

At Robinson's funeral, in New York City on Oct. 27, 1972, Harold (Pee Wee) Reese, a son of the South, was one of the pall bearers.

"I took it," Reese said, "as an honor."

~~~~~

This is a wonderful, moving, insightful, and evenhanded story. We get a different perspective of Jackie Robinson and learn a lot about Pee Wee Reese, including about his youth, career, and manner. But, mostly, I think we learn the way it was, so much so that this is more a profile of a time in America than of one person or another.

The story has a nice anecdotal lead drawn from Reese's youth and wonderful anecdotes from a life with the Dodgers that are woven into the rest of the story as well. Notice the choice use of verbs in this story, too: There's the one line where Robinson "groused" that opposing players were racists. A lesser writer would have simply said, "complained."

I hope you agree with that capsule analysis. Could you have produced a similar story yourself, though? You don't know Pee Wee Reese or any celebrities, you protest.

Well, it would be wonderful if we all had access to famous people, present and past. It would be wonderful if Queen Elizabeth II of England would allow you to shadow her for a couple of weeks, or give you unprecedented access to her daily routine. But it's not going to happen, I know. Students and beginning writers often complain that the really important people won't consent to interviews with little-known writers, and that's often true.

But wait a minute. A 78-year-old man recovering from cancer that I daresay most people reading this book never heard of is not really a celebrity. I firmly believe that someone like Reese would have spoken to a young reporter for a small paper or TV station as much as someone from *The New York Times*. Frankly, I doubt that he gets many calls for interviews anymore, and most people love to be interviewed.

And there was no problem getting "quotes" from the late Jackie Robinson, either. He was heavily quoted in his youth; Berkow just had to read up on him and give proper attribution as to where he retrieved the quotes.

I scanned several dozen stories dealing with Jackie Robinson and read a few all the way through before including the present one. What I like about Ira Berkow's story is that it does not take an obvious tack. The writer certainly recapitulates the story of Robinson and of the historic change in baseball he wrought. But mostly Berkow tells this well-known story through the eyes of another important player who is there with him; it was an alternative perspective.

Here are some particularly pleasing things about "At Robinson's Side": Reese's modest personality is captured by his repeated refusal to take much credit for helping Robinson in the early days. The hard segregationist sentiments of the era come through loud and clear when we learn of Dixie Walker's petition to keep Robinson off the field. Serious racial problems in the United States' past reverberate in the reference to the hanging tree in Brandenburg, Kentucky.

We learn how carefully Branch Rickey had to chart this plan to integrate Major League Baseball, yet we never feel as if we are being given a dry, stern, "politically correct" lecture.

We feel Robinson's pride and forceful personality, as well as his aggressive playing style and his consummate self-discipline in turning the other cheek during his first 2 years in "the bigs." We learn how Reese looks and dresses, and of his medical maladies in some detail; we even turn up

Reese's baseball statistics, but only at the end of a story. (These baseball stats were optional in a feature story that could have been read by a general audience.)

I also like Berkow's writing style. It's never pandering or florid, meaning too pretty or flowery. It shows a sensitivity to the times and the subject at hand. Note also how he handles a lot of his attribution. Students often ask me, "Do we have to say 'said' all the time?" That word probably *is* the best for attributing a quote. But sometimes a person can "recall." Berkow uses that word in his story. Sometimes they "reply." Berkow uses that form of attribution effectively, too.

And sometimes people note, speculate, reaffirm, or they "say with a sigh." So, you have lots of choices in terms of attributing quotes.

Now, imagine you are about to do a profile, yet you still worry that you don't know any famous people who are worth profiling. Wouldn't it be nice if there were a person on your college campus who has won a Nobel Prize? Or published 23 novels? No? Well, there probably are people of note just around the bend. Maybe you'll find someone who has the city's largest collection of Barbie dolls and costumes stuffed into a spare room at home? That's good enough for a little profile.

Perhaps there's a quadriplegic who's doing well in graduate school: You'll have a story of the indefatigable human spirit. (You'll also have a story dealing with disability issues, which is very timely.)

The first profile piece I ever sold, to the *Chicago Tribune Magazine*, was about an Irish barber on Chicago's Lincoln Avenue. He was surrounded by trendy bars and counterculture hangouts and was under pressure to move his old-fashioned business, even though he had been at the same location for years. I was charmed by the porcelain water basins in the middle of the shop's black and white ceramic tile floor; the high, pressed tin ceiling; and the genuine brass trim on the leather-upholstered barber chairs. Mostly, though, I was struck by the tapers.

Tapers are long candles, and this Irish-born barber, who had emigrated to the United States after World War II, used the tapers to singe customers' hair. *Singeing* was a medieval practice in which a barber would take the lit taper and hold it to the ends of the customer's hair, singeing it. The idea was that hair bleeds when you cut it, and singeing seals the hair. There was no scientific basis for this practice, but some customers still requested it, even in the 1970s, when I did the story.

The point is that lots of interesting people are not famous people. How did I find the guy with the tapers in the first place? Well, he was my barber. You just have to keep your eyes open, or read the smaller stories in your hometown newspaper. Jon Franklin likes to say he found the subject of his Pulitzer Prize-winning profile, "The Ballad of Old Man Peters," in a simple news story about a multilingual Black man who had been granted a community service award (Franklin, 1994). It was just a small magazine item that Franklin saw, but it made him think: What kind of octogenarian Black man in a poor neighborhood in Baltimore speaks Italian, anyway? Franklin chides the original writer for not knowing he had a great story on his hands. The complete story is reprinted in Franklin's (1994) own text, *Writing for Story*.

ASSIGNMENT

Your assignment is to look around you and find an interesting person, place, or thing to profile. Let's say it will be a person. Identify one or two outstanding things about this person that you think would make people want to read your story. Then call the person and suggest setting up an interview. Remember—you do not want to do a phone interview. You want to meet the person on his or her turf, and you may want to visit with the person two or three times, just to get to know the person better.

Let's say the person is a former nurse who went back to medical school and now is a well-known physician in the community. Maybe she's a heart specialist, cancer specialist, or advocate for early breast cancer detection. What's interesting about her story, beyond the fact that she's a successful physician, is that she fits at least one ideal of the modern women's movement, namely that women can break through traditional roles and raise their expectations for themselves, even if it means a midlife career change.

You would want to touch on the following in your interview:

- Early years.
- Job satisfaction and dissatisfaction as a nurse.
- Were her friends and family supportive of her return to medical school? And why did she want to become a doctor in the first place?
- Did she face any unusual hardships or discrimination in becoming a doctor? How was her acceptance?
- Does she consider herself a role model? What advice would she give to other women?
- How about her nonprofessional life? What does she do for recreation? Maybe she's an amateur artist or avid golfer? Maybe she sings in an informal "classic rock" group (OK, I know this is a bit of a stretch!).

You'll have to talk to friends and professional associates as well. What's she like, you'll ask them. But you'll also get wonderful little anecdotes and details from her life that she might not have brought up herself. You might also learn about problems that she was embarrassed to reveal: This kind of story is likely to be positive overall, but don't be afraid to report warts and all.

What's next for your profile subject? Your story will likely end with a look to the future. Is she looking for any new challenges? When does she plan on retiring?

I suggest you do the assignment in the following way, but your instructor (if you have one) may modify this:

1. Organize your notes on computer by theme; That is, have all the quotes and facts on "early years" in one section, on "family life" in another, and on "sexism" in another. Do this not just for your primary source, which is the profile subject herself, but for your secondary sources as well. (Note that you are not going to structure your story around a series of talking head sources; instead, you will structure your story around certain themes and stages in the profile subject's life.)

   Turn in these notes to your instructor, and listen if you're told to go back for additional interviewing or research.

2. Decide on a length for your story and try to stick to it. Typically for a daily newspaper feature your profile may be between 750 and 1,000 words—not a whole lot! A Sunday feature may be longer, and a magazine piece can be much, much longer, almost a small biography. Do a first draft, and give it to your instructor, or someone else who's willing to be tough on you! What questions are unanswered in your story? Where is the flow of the narrative choppy? Where do you lose the reader?

3. Go back and fill in the blank spaces in your draft, and rewrite it more clearly. Note I don't say to rewrite it more "beautifully." If you can write clear, easy-to-follow prose, and if you have something worthwhile to say, the last thing you have to worry about is whether your writing is "great." You will be a very successful writer even if you're not a great writer.

   Now, submit the revised story to your instructor again.

4. What if the teacher still doesn't like it? Consider further reporting and revising.

2

The Trend Story

"Trendy." It's a more controversial and ambiguous word than you think. We may want to dress in trendy fashions. (Hey, whatever happened to flannel shirts and Converse All-Star shoes?). Yet we put down people who are too trendy. Trendy people are shallow and insincere, we feel.

Trend pieces are among the most popular stories you'll see in the papers, though. By definition, a trend is something that's new, and what's new is news. Plus, the mere fact that certain things—sport utility vehicles, for example, or smoking by young people—are growing in popularity is proof enough that other people will read about these things.

Here's a good trend story from the respected *Boston Globe*. It's well researched and competently written. Most important, it follows precisely the format I want you to follow in doing your own trend stories: anecdotal lead that is really a clear example of the trend you're reporting, followed by a theme statement (known in the trade as a *nut graf*) that sums up the trend succinctly, followed by additional examples of the trend and quotes from authoritative sources explaining why the trend exists. Typically, you'll finish with the same person or example mentioned in the anecdotal lead.

The Boston Globe must have thought this was a fine story, otherwise they would not have run it on a Sunday front section in 1997. It was written by a part-timer, though. I've included it just because most of you reading this book could have produced a similar story: You could have identified the trend, found the subjects to interview, and written the story competently yourselves.

There's an old saying that "those who can, do, and those who can't, teach." The saying is an insult to the teaching profession, of course. But *The Boston Globe* tells of successful people from other professions who chose to give it all up, return to college for additional training and credentialing, and become school teachers. It's not a huge trend in U.S. society, but the writer, Marie Franklin, did spot it on the radar screen, and the story is successful. The story also is a good example of a partial focus structure, which we'll talk about more in a later chapter. For now let's just say that the author could not write about all teachers who come from other careers, so she focuses on just a few, and on one person more than any other. Let's read ...

~·~·~

The Lure of the Classroom*
by Marie C. Franklin

It was just before midcareer that Elizabeth Meyer took stock. A senior vice-president of an international real estate firm, she was 37, well paid, with offices and apartments in Boston and New York. Pulling down "in excess of $75,000 per year," Meyer said her job was to build and sell condominiums, adding that she was "on the road a lot."

Over time, the restlessness grew. "Then it started happening more often that I would come home from work after a 14-hour day and say 'so what,'" she recalled during a recent phone interview from the Dever School in Dorchester where, today, Meyer is a student teacher in a second-grade classroom.

Studying for a master's degree in education at Lesley College, Meyer said she planned her change from corporate to academic life. "About two years ago, I started to put money away, scale down my life and get ready for the change," she said.

"A lot of people told me I was crazy. But people really close to me said, 'This is where you should be,'" said Meyer.

The "this" is the classroom, where a growing number of adult career changers are showing up in school as Johnny's student teacher. Call them non-traditional learners, older teachers, corporate drop-outs or victims of downsizing, and the tag would probably stick. But what they really are, are adults, who—after one or more careers in the business world—gave it all up or took a job loss as a sign it was time for change, and returned to school to become teachers.

"Oh yes, there is definitely a trend, though no hard numbers," said William Dandridge, dean of the Education School at Lesley.

"The students entering our program are more mature and have lots of life experiences. Many transfer in from other careers, like law, banking and others," he said.

"These aren't people having midlife crises," Dandridge said. "They are people who have made deliberate choices and who are very serious about wanting to teach."

And nonplussed about the challenges that may be ahead.

---

*From The "Lure of the Classroom" by M. C. Franklin. Copyright © 1997, *The Boston Globe.* Reprinted by permission.

"I know I'll never make the kind of money in teaching I used to make in real estate," Meyer said, "but the quality of life matters more to me now."

"Feeling like I am doing something worthwhile, that I'm making a difference, is important, too," she said.

Meyer is not alone. Across the river at the University of Massachusetts at Boston, Colleen Connor, 36, is completing a master's degree in special education. Michael Mahoney, 39, is finishing his master's in elementary education. Mahoney left a career as a public relations director with a major Massachusetts supermarket chain. "Something important was missing," he said.

Connor, who taught for five years after graduating from the University of Connecticut in 1981, had left teaching to find a better paying job. "My father died and I had family obligations," said Connor. "Leaving teaching was the hardest thing I ever had to do."

Last September, Connor, who had spent the previous 10 years working as a paralegal, returned to education as a special-needs teacher at John Carver Elementary School in Carver. "I took a 50 percent pay cut," she said.

"At the law firm, I was paid a lot of money to push paper," she said. "But teaching is a job that matters, being with children, affecting their lives, that's what's important."

At the University of Massachusetts at Boston, where 278 graduate students in education make up the largest graduate program at the school, 75 percent of the students are adults. "They range from age 22 to 60 years old," said Denise Patmon, program director for the master's in teaching at UMass-Boston.

Patmon said there are many reasons for the surge in adults preparing to teach: corporate downsizing, education reforms, job prospects.

"Mergers in the '90s, slowing down of the high-tech industry, and other variables mean people are beginning to take a good look at their values, and making a deliberate choice to leave corporate positions to go into teaching or social service work," she said.

Patmon said education reform is also drawing newcomers to teaching. Education is elevated as a career when legislators and the public focus on improving working and learning conditions in the nation's schools, she said.

But Patmon said job prospects may be the most compelling lure.

"The projections are that we are facing the largest turnover of teachers at the turn of the century" than at any time in history, she said.

Already, California is experiencing a teacher shortage, she said. "I get regular calls from recruiters in California and also in Kansas City."

Even in Massachusetts, which has had a tight teaching job market for many years, "The situation is opening," according to Patmon, who predicts "a strong demand for teachers by the year 2000" in Massachusetts.

"We've been told informally that in Boston, they're expecting a sizable turnover the next five years," according to Dandridge of Lesley College.

Eighty percent of the recent master's in education graduates at UMass-Boston have found jobs teaching the last few years, "and many of them are in Massachusetts," according to Patmon.

Fred Andelman is a little less optimistic. He directs professional development at the Massachusetts Teachers Association and said that while there are spot shortages of teachers in the state due to population shifts, "On the whole, we don't see a looming demand for teachers over the next few years."

The shortages, he said, are in smaller, older towns such as Franklin, where there has been a building boom the last decade, or in small towns on Cape Cod and in south Worcester County "where housing is more affordable."

Another is the small South Shore town of Carver, where Colleen Connor found a teaching job this year.

"There was a pretty large class of new teachers who joined Carver this year," Connor said. "The town is growing because the train is coming here."

Like Carver, other towns in and near the Sliver Lake Regional School District, such as Kingston and Plymouth, are expecting growth during the next decade because the Old Colony Commuter Rail to Boston is expected by September. "I papered Massachusetts looking for a job," Connor said of her mail campaign to target 55 school systems. "I was asked to interview with five school systems," she said.

Connor's age and work experience outside education worked both ways while she was interviewing, she said.

"Some people were afraid that I'd been out of the field too long and that I wouldn't be up on the latest trends," Connor said, while others valued her newly acquired master's degree and her training in mediation.

"When I come to the table with parents, students or colleagues, I know how to resolve conflicts, and am a better listener, and I think that made me very attractive to school systems," she said.

Andelman noted two other trends affecting teacher job openings in the state: education reform and an aging teacher population.

He said many districts in Massachusetts have used state funds allotted under reform to restore teaching positions lost during the 1980s and Proposition 2 1/2. "Some of the teacher demand the last few years is related to reform."

When asked about speculation that an aging teacher population will result in widespread shortages during the next few years, Andelman said it hasn't yet.

"The teaching force is getting older, but the average age for teachers in Massachusetts is only around 50," he said.

"It's true, there is a large percentage of teachers either eligible for retirement now or in the near future, but the kind of pensions teachers are eligible for means many can't yet afford to retire," he said.

Ending her teaching career is the last thing on Elizabeth Meyer's mind. Right now, she's itching for a job in the classroom.

"I want to work in the Boston schools, but I'm willing to relocate. I'll go to Baltimore, Philly, California, anywhere they need teachers," Meyer said.

"I've got a long life ahead of me," she said, "and I want to do something I feel really good about."

Well, we know the phenomenon of business persons moving from the boardroom to the classroom is a trend because William Dandridge, dean of the Education School at Lesley College, calls it a "trend" in the sixth paragraph. Paragraph six is a veritable *nut graf* because the subject of the story has been summed up in a nutshell. (You could also argue the paragraph before the Dandridge quote is a nut graf, too, because that is where the author tells us in her own words that professionals from different backgrounds are turning to teaching careers.) The nut graf is important in any story, but it is especially so in a trend story. Whereas the anecdotal lead, which in this case is the little story of Elizabeth Meyer's experiences with a midlife career change, hints at the broader picture of other people with similar tales to tell, the nut graph absolutely, positively tells the reader the thrust of the story. Fairly high in your story—typically just after your anecdotal lead—you hit the reader with your nut graph. Franklin does it correctly here, right after introducing us to Elizabeth Meyer.

The importance of establishing the trend cannot be overemphasized. You, the writer, must prove that it's a trend involving many people! Otherwise, you have a profile story of Ms. Meyer, or a profile of the teaching profession, but not a trend story.

A trend emerges when you show any of the following:

- More people are doing this or that than ever before: More people are changing careers and becoming teachers than in the past; more people are living longer after a diagnosis of AIDS than previously was the case; more people are getting divorced these days; and so on.
- Fewer people are doing this or that than ever before: Fewer people are riding motorcycles than in the 1970s, when sales were at a peak; fewer people report having multiple sex partners than in the heyday of the sexual revolution; fewer people are saving for their retirement; and so on.

Typical trend stories include most of the stories you see in the daily business section (sales of sport utility trucks are up; profits at Coca-Cola are down; and so on); fashion stories (every spring and fall, like clockwork, you're going to read what's new in the fashion world); and plenty of music stories, too.

Lots of medical news is essentially trend reporting, as well. I recently wrote about a popular, new kind of laser eye surgery to correct nearsightedness, something I've lived with since I was 7 or 8.

Lots of people are having laser eye surgery these days. It's a new surgical technique originally perfected by a Russian doctor.

Do you see how this adds up to being a trend story?

Let's return to Franklin's teacher story. Note how she repeatedly answers the "why" question. Many of the quotes explain why people would change careers and take up teaching. Again, this helps prove that there is a trend. One "expert source," Denise Patmon of UMass-Boston, lists several objective reasons for the trend. This is all quite correct. If there's a trend, there must be a reason or reasons behind it, right?

Now, look at the line, "Meyer is not alone," about one-quarter of the way through the story. This one, simple sentence is what's known as the *transition*. It's important in any story to keep the reader moving from one section of the story to another (think of the old line, "Meanwhile, back at the ranch ... "). But transitions are extremely important in trend stories. It's where you show the reader that your story is not a mere profile; it's not about one person or an isolated case. It's about a trend: "Meyer is not alone."

The author, Franklin, could also have written, "Meyer is one of thousands ... " or, "Across the country, midcareer professionals like Meyer are chucking their corporate suits for a crack at the chalkboard...." It would be the same thing: Meyer is representative of a trend; she's not alone.

Other transitions exist in the story, to move you from one section to another or to introduce an alternate point of view. Look at the line that begins, "Fred Andelman is a little less optimistic ..." about job prospects for midcareer teachers. That one line is a transition, meant to show that not everyone agrees with the rosy picture the author has been presenting so far, and to introduce an opposing point of view. Transitions are a bit like the "theme sentences" you were taught to write at the start of each paragraph when you were in public school. Most important, transitions bridge one section of a story with the next.

Now, look more deeply into the story. There's the claim that 75% of 278 graduate students in education at one Massachusetts college are "adults." This statistic, albeit a little cumbersome, is offered as proof that a trend really exists here.

The author reinforces the notion of a trend near the end of the story as well. This is where she quotes a source who speaks of "two other trends affecting teacher job openings in the state: education reform and an aging teacher population." The story goes on to prove, or at least argue credibly, that these related trends also are authentic. One special feature of any trend story is indeed to prove to the reader that the trend is authentic.

Imagine you were writing a story about the upsurge in teen smoking. You'd need some credible statistics comparing latest smoking data with older data to show the change, wouldn't you?

"The Lure of the Classroom" is a fundamentally sound story in another regard. Note the first person quoted in this story, and the last. It's one and the same person. Elizabeth Meyer, the jet-set real estate wiz with homes in Boston and New York, who gave up $75,000 a year to become a teacher, is quoted in both places.

This is a common journalistic technique: You end a story where you began. This provides a nice feeling of unity and summing up of your theme, and it reinforces the focus aspect of your story.

I've seen this technique of beginning and ending with the same person in a story called by at least two different names. One is the *sandwich technique*, as if you are wrapping your story between two pieces of bread. As in a sandwich, the meat of the story goes in the middle. Your lead and the ending are pieces of the same bread.

This technique also is closely related to the *Q shape* of a story. Imagine the letter Q as if it were a circle, but with that little squiggle exiting in the bottom right quadrant. Now, imagine you begin your story by that little squiggle or line, go all the way around until you end up at exactly the point where you began, and then exit the story at that point. That's the Q shape, and it's often used for historical tales, where you have to go back in time to fill in a lot of missing or background information, and you finally come back to where you started a story.

Think of any story on adult survivors of child sexual abuse, for example. The story begins with a happy, well-adjusted adult, or perhaps with the adult in therapy. Then the story goes back in time to the terrible events that befuddled the subject's life in the first place, followed by years of unhappiness and efforts at therapy, and then the confrontations between adult child and accused parent. Finally, the story ends right where it began, with the very same scene in which the subject was first introduced to the reader.

What we call this technique is not important, though; it's the technique itself I want you to understand.

"The Lure of the Classroom" is not beyond reproach, however. The author is almost fawning over her subjects, for one thing. Whereas you can be sympathetic and well disposed toward your subjects, the line should be drawn short of simply packaging and promoting them, as if you were part of a marketing scheme. Franklin commits no egregious sin in this regard, and she does acknowledge that at least some career-change teachers were forced into it by the labor market, but overall she goes further in celebrating her subjects than I would have. You can see this in the plethora of high-minded quotes she attributes to her teacher sources in the story.

And the story is a bit weak in terms of "color" or visualization. The author tries to set a scene and paint a picture in the lead—we do have at least a mental picture of what Elizabeth Meyer's life was like before she became a teacher—but there's not a whole lot of color beyond this. The author didn't do enough observing, in other words, which would have provided those all-important visual details. In fact, the author violates one of my pet rules by doing a phone interview with Elizabeth Meyer, her primary subject, instead of visiting her at the Dever School where she was teaching. Remember: You must be the eyes and ears of the reader. You are the reader's agent and advocate and servant. Give the reader a good ride for his or her money, if you can.

But this is all mild criticism. Franklin has written a clear, valid, and useful trend story that follows the format I want you to learn.

Here's another trend story, one that's based on the old, old notion of "mail-order brides."

In early 1996 I received a call from Bob Malcomb, a guy who lived near Louisville, Kentucky. Malcomb said he had just been to Russia to meet the woman he might marry one day. She'd be coming to the United States soon and would I like to meet her, he wondered aloud?

Hmm, I thought.

We had fun with this one in the office, especially the women: What kind of person would travel to a foreign country to find a bride, they all asked.

Actually, several of us were aware of this trend. There had been a steady stream of Korean, Filipino, and Taiwanese women into the United States, women who probably could be called "mail- order brides." What was new here was that the women of Russia and other former Soviet bloc countries were now part of the mix.

Normally, we do not do stories on people who call and ask us to do stories on them or their family members. Typically these are moms promoting a teenager who just won a beauty pageant down at the mall, or some guy who wants to show us his restored 396SS Chevelle. (Well, I'd actually look at a car like that, but I'm not sure I'd do a story on it.) But Russian brides?

Hmm, I thought again. My editor, Ruth, gave me the green light.

I decided to write about Bob Malcomb after everything he told us checked out, that is, after I called some agencies that deal with foreign brides and confirmed all the details he related to me. We also discovered that Malcomb was a homeowner with a good job in engineering, which added some credibility.

In truth, I wrote this story mostly because it promised to be fun. As far as trends go, this was not a big one. But I organized this story in very much the same way Franklin structured her teacher story—and Marie Franklin and I had never met! My trend story included:

- A focus or primary subject, especially in the lead and ending.
- A nut graf and transition that tells the reader, "The individual cited above is part of a trend."
- Other examples of the trend.
- Expert sources, which are used to provide reasons why the trend exists. (Other trend stories might have more numbers and statistics to back up the trend; I just have a couple of statistics.)
- Observation, which provides a few visual details to dress up the story.
- An ending, which simply goes back to the focus in the beginning of the story.

I included this story, in part, because I like it. But it's yet another story that anyone reading this book could have produced. The subjects are not famous; the trend is not something limited to trendy people in New York or San Francisco; you would not have needed a hefty expense account to do your research.

~~~

Russian to the Altar: American Men Extend Hands Across the Sea, Seeking Hands in Marriage*
By Abe Aamidor

Meet Bob Malcomb, lonely guy.

An engineer by trade, he says all the guys he works with are just that—guys.

And though he belongs to a singles group at church, he's seen the same three or four women there since Ronald Reagan was president.

So, how's a lonely guy supposed to find a wife? For Malcomb, 39, the solution lay in traveling 8,000 miles to the Cosmos Hotel in Moscow, Russia, for his most recent date. There, he met dozens of eligible young women at a "social" arranged by a Russian-American introduction service.

Today? Malcomb is engaged to Olga Nickolaevna Sorokina, a 28-year-old nurse from a small town outside of Moscow. She arrived in early March.

Sorokina and her five-year-old daughter, Dasha, live in a room addition Malcomb built behind the house he shares with his mother. While everybody gets to know each other better, Sorokina has her own microwave oven, washing machine and loft bed.

"She's got 90 days," said Malcomb, who lives in tiny Deputy, Ind., a town so small it doesn't appear on most maps. "Then she's got to go back to Russia if we don't get married."

*From "Russian to the Altar: American Men Extend Hands Across the Sea, Seeking Hands in Marriage" by A, Aamidor. Copyright © 1996, *The Indianapolis Star*. Reprinted by permis-

Increasingly, American men are turning to Russian-American introduction services to find wives, say people who run such agencies.

Many men who use foreign introduction services live in small towns
or isolated areas. The white American men who use the Russian services say they prefer women of the same race.

David Besuden, a Kentucky insurance agent who met his Russian
wife, Elena, through such a service, liked the results so much he
started his own company.

Now, the Besudens run Anastasia International out of a Winches-
ter, Ky., office. Anastasia, named for the legendary lost daughter of the
last Russian czar, publishes magazines with photographs of Russian
women, sells their addresses to interested men at about $10 a head,
and leads tours to Russia to meet the women in person.

"The women come from all over," Besuden said. "We've had
women come from as far as Siberia to meet American and Cana-
dian men."

Besuden is taking 26 men to Russia in June. He says that on his
most recent trip more than 30 women were waiting outside the hotel
for the tour bus to arrive on a Thursday afternoon, even though the big
"social" wasn't scheduled until the following evening.

Russian-American introductory services are promoted in a host of
publications and through various matchmaker services. The Russian
women generally can advertise for free and typically supply their own
photographs, a few biographical details, sometimes including physical measurements, and a quote or statement. A few describe themselves as "Christian," which is what Malcomb says attracted him to
Sorokina as much as her youth and good looks.

The magazines look like a cross between a high school yearbook
and a holiday gift catalog.

Most of the women indicate they're marriage-minded; many say
older men are no problem (most of the women are in their 20s), but
many others impose a minimum height requirement: Five-foot-eight is
about as low as they'll go.

Some of the ads seem inexplicable. "I am calm, modest, trusting,
shy," writes 21-year-old Julia, but her picture shows her leaning over
the edge of a powerboat on the Black Sea, wearing a tiny bikini.

Nearly half got engaged

Malcomb went to Russia for several days in September, then returned in November. He says women outnumbered men eight to one
at the "social" he attended.

He and Sorokina, with whom he had corresponded for several
months before agreeing to meet her in person, went off to a nearby
coffee shop and spoke through an interpreter for several hours. He ultimately met her parents, her younger brother and her daughter from a
previous marriage; the Sorokinas all lived together in a smallish apartment about 40 miles from Moscow.

Nine of the 20 men on his September tour came back engaged, says Malcomb. But some inevitably committed a *faux pas* or two.

"Some of the guys brought photos of their houses to impress the women, but they weren't impressed. The Russian women wanted to know if their wives all left them because they were tired of cleaning house."

Why do so many Russian women want to become American wives?

"The prime motivation for 90 percent of the women is that they do not want to marry a Russian man, or a Ukranian, or anyone from the former USSR," said Lawrence Holmes, a La Jolla , Calif., immigration attorney. "The reason is that the Russian men have three things against them—they're alcoholic, at least by our standards; they're lazy; and they're very rough on their women physically. But these are all generalizations."

Galena Alger, a 27-year-old Russian national who met her husband while working as a tour guide on a ship, says some women come to the West for economic and educational opportunity, but that most are looking for a better mate than they think they can find at home.

"There are different men in Russia, but they are getting worse," said Alger, who now works for Scanna International, an Atlanta-based introduction service with customers worldwide.

The American men who employ these services fit a narrow profile, agency operators suggest. Often in their late 30s or early 40s, they somewhat disproportionately come from small rural communities.

"We have lots of cowboys," said Barbara Lauter Holt, operations manager for Scanna International.

The male customers claim to have trouble meeting eligible women at home, though Malcomb candidly admits there's another reason behind the move. "They haven't heard of women's liberation in Russia," he said with a chuckle.

90 days of grace

Immigration lawyer Holmes says he's helped 500 Russian and former Soviet Bloc women obtain K-1 "fianceé visas" and come to America in the last five years. U.S. law requires that the women be engaged to an American and provide evidence that they actually know the man they're coming over to marry, such as a photograph shot within the last two years showing the two together, though there are exceptions.

And the marriage has to take place within 90 days of arrival or the visa expires.

Men who try to find a Russian bride this way should expect to pay at least $7,000 in travel and legal costs to bring the woman to these shores. Malcomb says he's paid more than $8,000 so far, including his two trips to Russia, bringing Sorokina and her daughter over, and legal fees.

Move angered some

Olga Nicolaevna Sorokina has been in America about two weeks now. She does not speak English well, but indicated that Malcomb's family and friends have been kind to a fault: She, Dasha and Malcomb have been guests for dinner virtually every evening since she's arrived, and neighbors recently took her and her daughter horseback riding.

Malcomb's mother, Lelia, at first opposed the idea of importing a wife from Russia, but now says she's fond of Olga and Dasha.

Yet there are those in Jennings County and elsewhere in southern Indiana who are up in arms at what Malcomb's done, he says. "The postmaster out here was really angry when she heard I was bringing in Olga. 'Aren't there enough women here?' she asked."

"And over at the church I go to in Louisville a woman asked if she could see my book (of potential brides); then she locked it up in her car and wouldn't give it back."

Malcomb and Sorokina have not set a date for the wedding. It may be the engineer in his personality coming through, but the marriage is in the developmental stage and Malcomb wants to get the bugs out before committing to full production.

In the meantime, playful little Dasha watches Walt Disney videos and her mother tap dances with her fingers across the computerized Russian-English dictionary she employs.

But Malcomb is happy so far.

"I got into this because I was playing a joke on my brother, who has a barber shop nearby," he says. "I was reading a Christian singles magazine and they had all these ads for 'Meet Korean women' and 'Meet Filipino women' and 'Meet Russian women.' I saw Olga's picture and she was so pretty. I decided to write away myself."

The focus of the story is Malcomb, or Malcomb and Sorokina. The experts are the agents and lawyers who make all the arrangements. The proof of the existence of the trend in part comes from statements by the experts, but also from immigration numbers (recall the lawyer who says he's processed 500 "fianceé visas" himself in the last five years).

Can you spot the nut graf and transition in "Russian to the Altar"?

It's in the eighth paragraph: "Increasingly, American men are turning to Russian-American introduction services to find wives, say people who run such agencies."

That is what the story is about, and the word "increasingly" clearly puts Malcomb in a pool of people who are doing the same thing as he.

Malcomb is not alone (to borrow a phrase from *The Boston Globe* teacher story). Malcomb is one of hundreds of men who.... All across America men like Malcomb are turning to.... Increasingly, American men are turning to....

This story has a number of quotes as well, but not too many. I always go for punchy, colorful, or just plain funny quotes in my features. If I'm merely citing facts and figures or basic information—*Most men who do this are in their 30s or 40s and live in Rural America*, or, *Malcomb and Sorokina corresponded for several months before meeting*—there is no reason to use an actual quote. You might as well paraphrase, summarize, condense.

Remember: You, not the persons you're interviewing, are the writer. The basic rule on quoting people is this: If a source can say something more colorfully or cleverly or cogently than you can, then by all means quote him or her. If the person's personality comes through in a quote, then quote away. In all other cases, don't.

By the way, can I give you a preview of the legitimate use of "point of view" in feature writing, albeit in a nonpolitical vein? Look again at the paragraph where I write about 21-year-old Julia, the "shy, modest, trusting" young lady who just happens to knock 'em dead in her itsy bitsy, teeny weeny, little bikini on the Black Sea. I'm clearly impugning her by describing her sultry photograph; I'm clearly telling the reader, "I don't believe it." Any objections?

Changing lifestyles are good sources of trend stories. Look at high school or college students today: Are there any abstinence clubs in your area? They may not go by this name, but increasingly young people are saying no to the sexual revolution and are adhering to abstinence, because of concerns about unwanted pregnancies and abortion, and/or fear of sexually transmitted diseases including AIDS. And, some must be motivated by old-fashioned morality issues. Talk to people who adopted abstinence—who are they, why are they doing this, and so on—and you'll have a trend story.

By the same token, you may find senior citizens who are moving in together. This would have been called "shacking up" when they were youths in the 1940s or 1950s, but there is very little stigma left concerning unmarried adults becoming sexually intimate. Talk about role reversals! Anyway, this is another trend story.

How about retirees who sell their homes—those 4-bedroom split-levels where they raised their kids—and travel year-round across the country in 40-foot-long Winnebago motor homes? Many such people have no permanent home address anymore. Are they 70-year-old hippies? Not really, but they do collectively constitute a trend. According to the Good Sam Club, about 100,000 Americans live like this, following the sun from one RV campsite to another (Aamidor, 1997). Phone some campsites, RV clubs, or motor home manufacturers in your area for leads on people to interview.

The following trend may be passé by the time you read this book, but today there are plenty of young people with rings through their noses, tongues, navels and—so I've been told—other fairly intimate body parts. Trend story!

Tobacco: Smoking is up among White teens, but down among African American youth. Why? This should be a good trend story for a few more years.

And, for you college students reading this book: Why does it now take many students 5 years or longer to finish undergraduate school? Call your local registrar and some national association of colleges to establish that this trend really exists; then start interviewing students and administrators as to why this is happening. What hardships is this trend creating (such as crowded or "filled" classrooms)? What can be done to stop it? (Some state scholarships at state schools now are limited to 4 years, so you better graduate in time.) Answer these questions and you'll have a rich trend story.

ASSIGNMENT

I want you to write a trend story using the following basic outline. This is not the only way to write a trend story, but master this simple technique and I guarantee you that you'll be miles ahead of most of your peers.

1. Anecdotal lead, in which you focus on one person, group, or example of the trend in question.
2. Nut graf, which means you say in plain English what the trend is.
3. Transition, wherein you tell the reader that the person or persons highlighted in your lead "are not alone." (You often can reverse the order of II and III or combine the two steps.)
4. Additional examples of the trend.
5. Expert testimony and statistics to back up the existence of the trend. (This may be reversed or even mingled with IV).
6. Ending, in which you go back to the person or persons introduced in your lead and give some resolution to their particular stories.

Note that the outline doesn't merely direct you on how to organize or structure your story; it provides a reporting plan as well, directing you to certain types of sources for your information in the first place.

I suggest that you count on doing at least two drafts of your story. If you're doing this exercise for a feature writing class, whether in a college or adult education setting, I suggest you be given two distinct deadlines.

3

The Pro and Con Story

Give both sides of the story.

Probably no other common sense wisdom is more enshrined in traditional U.S. journalism.

Think of election coverage. Newspapers that give more play to one major candidate than another or consistently produce more positive stories about one candidate's policies and "issues" will quickly be suspected of biased coverage.

Controversial topics, too, require fair treatment of "both sides" of the question. Many large cities in recent years have wrestled with the question of offering large financial incentives to professional sports teams in the hopes of keeping them in town or luring them away from other cities. In 1984, the city of Indianapolis, Indiana, won the Colts away from Baltimore, Maryland, by building a new, domed stadium. But in 1996, Baltimore grabbed the Browns from Cleveland, Ohio. And so it goes.

Some people are disgusted that taxpayer money is used to entice and reward such professional sports franchises. After all, if you want to support your "local" team, you can buy tickets, these critics argue. The tax money could better be used for schools, roads, or health care for the poor. Or the tax rates could be lowered.

Yet city administrators talk about the "economic impact" of having a professional sports franchise in town. There are tourist dollars to be spent; there are the restaurant meals that will be sold before and after the game; there's the revitalization of depressed downtown areas they believe a new sports stadium and team will bring.

Who's right, and who's wrong? You—the writer—give both sides of the story and let the reader decide.

Another, more dynamic way of looking at pro-and-con stories is in terms of "should" and "should not." By this I mean that proponents of either side of a controversial issue often are recommending that something should, or should not, be done. You'll read a story shortly about the fate of a historic building in Indianapolis: One side in the debate says it should be preserved; the other says it should not be saved, but rather demolished to make way for new business. Stories with two sides that involve actually doing something, or doing one thing over another, provide a natural dynamic that makes them easy to write and easy to read.

Pro and con stories are bread-and-butter stories for daily journalists, but we see many stories that are in effect one-sided (such as those supporting donations to a United Way agency, without investigating whether such and such agency deserves more support than another; those supporting educational reform, without challenging whether one reform program is better than another; and those opposing a deer kill in a local state park, without fully looking at the issue of deer overpopulation). Yet fair is fair. You should give both sides of an issue (or more, if necessary).

Later in this book we'll look at *advocacy journalism* (in chap. 8, on point of view) in which the journalist takes a side, arguing that one position is correct, often while trying to put down any opposition. This is a controversial practice in U.S. journalism that has been with us for at least 30 years. Even if you believe there is room for advocacy journalism, there still will be many, many stories that have to be reported and interpreted in a balanced way. The reader will need to hear both sides of the issue to make an informed decision. This is a concession usually made by the modern adherents of what is variously known as *public journalism* or *civic journalism*: You, the journalist, must present the reader with a range of solutions to the pressing problems of the day, not merely lead the cheer for one side or another.

There's an additional reason to be evenhanded: Pro-and-con stories are easy to write and can be interesting to read. Without a doubt you'll have sources from both sides plying you with all kinds of data and facts to support "their" side. You never will be short of material to work with.

Furthermore, because pro-and-con stories tend to deal with controversial topics, readers may either hate you or love you for what you write, but they likely will respect you for being fair. In general, controversial topics will have ardent supporters on both sides of the issue (just think of the ongoing abortion debate). Touch a nerve close to their hearts and you will have dedicated readers from your lead sentence to the last period, but you will lose half of your audience if you're not fair.

Sometimes a pro-and-con story includes information that has a down side, such as a story that introduces a new procedure or drug. You must report all risks associated with, say, a new antidepressant or perhaps refractive laser eye surgery. Risks or contraindications are listed on package labeling for over-the-counter drugs; you should do no less in your reporting.

I did a story several years ago for *The Indianapolis News* on the growing popularity of cosmetic facial surgery (Aamidor, 1987), even for ordinary, middle-income people. I included two brief caveats or disclaimers deep in the text, indicating that there's always the risk of infection and that even successful surgeries will leave patients feeling like someone has just rubbed their epidermis off with sandpaper. I thought I was being fair and responsible in doing this.

The mother of a fellow reporter, largely on the basis of reading my story, elected to have such cosmetic facial surgery. She had a terrible experience, though. She needed a constant supply of pain killers for more than a month, and her face was so puffy, raw, and red after the surgery she would not go out in public for weeks. The woman's son asked if I had not warned readers of the risks inherent in the surgery.

I looked at my story again, and indeed I had. Not once, but twice. Yet both disclaimers were really quite small and buried deep in the story. I felt sorry for the woman and was determined then and there to disclose more clearly in future stories any risks involved with any medical procedure or drug I was writing about.

Here's an example of a pro-and-con story that any of you might have been assigned, and that any of you could have done well. It's a story that grew out of *beat* coverage, of zoning issues in the central city in Indianapolis. The issue is whether or not to tear down a historic building in Indianapolis and put up a modern drug store in its place. The problem reminds me a little of folk singer Joni Mitchell's lyric, "They paved paradise and put up a parking lot."

No, there was no virgin timber at stake at 38th and College Streets in Indianapolis in 1992. There was a depressed neighborhood with a two-story walk-up office building that for the most part stood empty. The Chinese restaurant sign in front was broken (the restaurant itself was long gone) and *The Indianapolis News* ran a large photo with the story showing an abandoned car parked illegally right on the sidewalk in front of the building. To some people, this whole scene screamed "urban renewal," especially when Walgreen, a national drug store chain, said they'd buy the property from its current owner, clear the lot, and put up a modern store.

But historic preservationists cried foul. The old, nearly abandoned building was distinctive architecturally; some even claimed it was beautiful, although that's a matter of taste, I suppose. In any case, could't the original building be rehabilitated, then converted to small offices and shops for neighborhood people to staff and take pride in?

~.~´~

Storefront Politics*
by Abe Aamidor

It's a clash between "progress" and "history."

On one side are the MaCo Building's owner, a local developer, and most of the areas's residents, all of whom want to see the better part of the art deco-inspired structure at 38th Street and College Avenue demolished in favor of a new, suburban-style Walgreen Drug Store and parking lot.

The store will mean 20 to 25 jobs and increased security for the blighted intersection. A couple of viable businesses share the corner with an abandoned gas station, vacant supermarket and shuttered bar and grill, not to mention the nearly empty MaCo Building itself, formerly home to the Mandarin Inn restaurant.

On the other side of the issue are historic preservationists who point to delicate, limestone relief sculptures in the MaCo Building's walls, its beveled art-glass windows and its pressed steel roof over a tower room.

It's unusual in Indianapolis, and besides, argue the preservationists, leveling the MaCo Building would violate the neighborhood's 38th Street Corridor plan, which calls for saving historic buildings wherever possible.

A vote by the Metropolitan Development Commission Wednesday may seal the fate of the building. If the planning commission approves a petition to rezone residential property just south of an alley behind the MaCo Building and include it in the proposed development, a deal to sell the building will go through. The old structure—except for a wing that now houses a coin laundry—will be flattened.

Mike Quinn, attorney for Continental Realty and Development Co., who will develop the property and lease it to Walgreen, says the building's architecture may appeal to some, but that the small, cubicle-like offices, high ceilings and walk-up second floor make it unsuitable for commercial purposes today. "The people who think the city is one big park don't understand that," Quinn said.

David Frederick, director of the Indianapolis office of Historic Landmarks Foundation of Indianapolis, says the MaCo Building is eligible for historic landmark status, though it is unlikely the building could be designated as such without the active support of its owner. Landmark status would add a layer of protection to the building and make it more difficult to destroy.

"I just think it's short-sighted to demolish the building," said Frederick."I could show you 100 slides of buildings built in the '60s and '70s

---

*From "Storefront Politics" by A. Aamidor. Copyright © 1992, *The Indianapolis News*. Reprinted by permission. (This story has been edited for inclusion in this collection).

and even '80s that tore down important resources and now have gone out of business."

Even the plan to put in a new drug store has irked people who express no affinity for the Maco Building's art and history. "Really, it doesn't bother me that they'll tear it down," said neighborhood resident Darwin Bell while folding clothes in the laundry in the eastern wing of the building. "But they need to put in a grocery store, not a drug store."

What's in a name?

The MaCo Building—its name is an amalgam of Maple Road, an early name for part of 38th Street, and College Avenue—was developed as a market with adjoining office space and a two-story "tower" at the corner. Ironically, the Walgreen Drug Co.—the same company that wants the building torn down—was one of the first occupants.

The building's recent history has been sorry. A record shop, second-hand furniture store and beauty shop, as well as the Mandarin Inn, have all closed or moved, and a combined travel agency and beauty store rents space on a month-to-month lease.

"The other businesses were just barely surviving," said Peter Chung, who manages the travel agency. "The rent was just right, but the people in the neighborhood were not cooperating. There was a lot of shoplifting."

Peter Pappas, who operates the unrelated MaCo Dry Cleaners a half-block west, said he, too, is fearful of crime. "To be honest, it's very dangerous around here," said Pappas, who has operated his business in what was once a movie theater since 1958. "Not my customers, but they're not the ones that are dangerous."

Dave Leonards, past president of the Mapleton Fall Creek Neighborhood Association, said most residents of the area favor the return of Walgreen's.

"We're faced with progress vs. history," said Leonards. "The neighborhood has looked at it and said in this particular situation the benefits Walgreen's is going to bring outweigh the value of the building."

"Plus, the feeling is if this building is so important, where was everyone when the Chinese restaurant closed?"

Continental attorney Mike Quinn also challenges people trying to save the building.

"They've got nothing at stake here," said Quinn, speaking of the Historic Landmark Foundation. "They don't own the building and they don't live in the neighborhood."

The bottom line

Historic Landmark's David Frederick defends his group's interest in the building.

"There are other values here in the world besides the bottom line," said Frederick, who promises to be at the planning commission hearing, along with other preservationists. "There are other things that make a city beautiful. I'm not convinced that this building can't meet some economic needs."

Frederick pointed to Coburn Place, an old public school building converted to assisted-living housing less than two blocks away on 38th Street, and the creation of an O'Malia's Food Market in the former Sears store Downtown as two ways old buildings can be put to new uses.

Other supporters of the status quo include Bill Connor, a board member of the neighborhood association and president of William S. Connor Inc., a general contractor specializing in remodeling and restoration work. Noting that one objection to saving the building is the walk-up second floor, Connor estimated that an elevator could be installed for $40,000.

"I think it's a shame to lose that building," said Connor. "There are very few like it in Indianapolis. Its art deco motifs present some styling that you just don't see. Secondly, it's structurally sound and seems to me it would be a waste of resources to flatten it."

The sale price is unknown, but Kipp Normand of Historic Landmarks says the building previously was offered at $295,000. The owner, Stanley Cohen, could not be reached for comment.

Quinn says the estimated cost of the Walgreen's project, including demolishing most of the MaCo Building, is $1 million.

As presently zoned, the owner or developers can do pretty much what they will with the building, as long as they don't go beyond the alley behind it. While the plan to destroy the historic building would seem to be an apparent contradiction of the non-binding 38th Street Corridor plan, Maury Plambeck, a senior planner with the Department of Metropolitan Development, said the major objection to the plan is the "setback," or how far the building will be from the street. The original site plan for the new store was being revised this week, said Quinn.

The city has become involved in the case because of the petition to rezone adjoining residential property, which would then be included in the Walgreen's development.

Feeling in the Mapleton Fall Creek area is that the MaCo Building soon will be history, and not in the way the preservationists want. Wendell Purchase, president of the association, said the community held several meetings last fall and that the majority of people expressed support for the proposed development.

"One of our neighbors said, 'If Benjamin Harrison had slept there, it might be historic. But he not only didn't sleep there, he didn't even shop there,'" recalled Purchase. "A lot of people really don't know what historic means. It means different things to different people."

~~~

You'll have a separate chapter on quotes in the last section of this book, but I have to point out here attorney Mike Quinn's opening quote: "The people who think the city is one big park don't understand" how little economic utility the MaCo Building has in the current business climate.

Them's fightin' words! It's a quote with attitude, not merely a summary of the man's position.

There are other good quotes in this story, although they don't start coming hot and heavy until well into the story. Young reporters either use too many quotes or no quotes at all in their stories. Too many quotes early in a story confuse the reader and lead to the dreaded "talking heads" or "popping heads" syndrome, where you really don't know who is talking or what their authority or place in the story is. In general, though, you only quote people when it's a really punchy or vivid quote or if what they say so succinctly sums up a position that you, the professional writer, could not have said it better yourself.

Note how clearly the problem is laid out in the opening paragraphs. Famous writing coach and lecturer Don Fry (personal communication, 1995) likes to talk about the "airport terminal" test for local news coverage. Can a reader, just arriving by plane in a new city, pick up the local paper and understand what's going on in a particular story just on the basis of what he or she reads in that day's coverage of events? The answer here would be a resounding "yes." There's a lot to be said for clarity, you know.

Note also how the coverage is pretty balanced in this story, although you might say it's slightly weighted toward the supporters of economic progress. Yet that wouldn't reflect my bias. The fact is there was more support to tear down the building and put up a drug store, so it would have been artificial to provide exactly 50% of the space for one side of the issue and 50% for the other side. There is no formula for these things, though. I cannot claim that if 90% of the sentiment were to, say, hang a convicted child molester who just moved into the neighborhood that 90% of your coverage should reflect such a sentiment. You'll have to decide on a case-by-case basis; it's the principle of giving balanced coverage that's more at stake here than a word count.

I want you to pay particular attention to the types of sources here. Normally you have two types of sources in a story: expert sources and what I call "human interest" or "real people" sources. The experts have (or should have) the data, the background, and the objectivity to help explain things in your story. The real people are those people actually affected by the news.

Think of a tornado story: Surely you would talk to people who lost their homes or to survivors of a deadly attack? How do they feel? How will they rebuild their lives?

You'd also talk to meteorologists who can explain how and why this latest storm did its damage. You would talk to a banker or economist who could explain the dollars and cents impact of the storm on the larger community.

The above story blurs the difference somewhat between expert and ordinary source. That's because in controversies (and this is a controversy, which is why it was written as a pro-and-con story) almost everybody you want to quote is affected by the issues. Investors, lawyers, neighborhood residents—they all have a stake in the outcome. Having said that, there is a very nice mix of sources in this story, from a guy folding his laundry in part of the building that may survive demolition to well-heeled preservationists to at least one truly neutral, informed source in the city administration who helped me understand the technical zoning issue at stake.

I said at the beginning of this story that pro-and-con stories are easy to write. Why? It's easy to identify the players, for one thing. Figuring out who to interview in a lot of stories can be tough. You're going to be on a deadline, even in features, and you can't afford to spin your wheels too much. Just look at who's affected by the news; just look at whomever has a stake in the outcome. This will give you all the sources you need and will provide you with some impassioned quotes as well.

Also, get out of the office! This has been said before, but it can't be stressed too much. I cannot imagine having done this story successfully without visiting the MaCo Building. I went there twice, in fact: once, to talk to neighborhood residents and business people whom I knew would be available for interviews during the day, the second time with a couple of historic preservationists who gave me a tour of the building and pointed out just what was nice about it.

An outline for this kind of story is a snap.

1. Statement of problem, including both sides of the issue.
2. One side of the issue in greater depth.
3. The other side of the issue at length.
4. History of the problem; additional quotes, data, sources; complicating factors.
5. The ending, which may look to the future (and often show you a big, fat question mark, metaphorically speaking), and which often will do so with a sharply worded quote from one of the players quoted earlier in the story.

By the way, what do you think happened to the MaCo Building? I'd like to print the answer upside down in small print at the bottom of the page, like they always do in puzzles and quizzes. Let's just say the MaCo Building really is history now, or, they did pave paradise and put up a parking lot.

ASSIGNMENT

This is obvious. Find a local controversy. It can be one of the big issues of the day (pro-choice vs. right-to-life), but I'd rather you pick something more mundane, such as "landfill vs. incinerator" for disposing of garbage or a controversy over putting in a halfway house for the mentally ill in a middle-class residential neighborhood (this is always good for getting ordinary people agitated). You can use the outline I gave above, or develop a more detailed one. Make sure you understand both sides of the issue (for this exercise, try to stick to just two sides of an issue) before you attempt to write anything. Identify the people who are affected by the issue and/or care about it and interview them, and make sure you do on-site reporting. For example, if there is a controversy over any kind of halfway housing in your community (for ex-prisoners, battered women, runaway teens, etc.), go visit the proposed site and talk to neighbors. Go visit the landfill and/or incinerator if you're doing the garbage disposal story (don't laugh; many of you will have to do such a story within your first year on the job as a newspaper reporter).

Do a draft and give it to your instructor; revise as he or she directs, which probably will involve shortening your story while doing more reporting.

4

The News Peg

As I'm sitting here writing this chapter, the local TV news is reporting yet another high-speed police chase in the Indianapolis area. In the movies, about 200 cars can be crashed before the bad guy finally spins out of control and ends up in a ditch, only scratched and slightly dazed. Cut to the next scene, and some uniformed cops are carting him off in handcuffs while a salty, old detective who chased the suspect down (Gene Hackman? Steve McQueen?) is making eyes at his female partner.

In the real world, though, these chases often end up in fatalities, frequently involving innocent victims. Here's the kernel of a really good news feature, from a small item carried in *The Indianapolis Star* on August 13, 1997: "According to the U.S. Department of Transportation's National Highway Traffic Safety Administration, 377 people died last year in high-speed chases involving police." (Staff report, *The Indianapolis Star*, 1997)

This may sound cynical to you, but police chases are a gold mine for copy. I did a computer search (on my newspaper's computer) using the simple keywords "high speed chase" and came up with specific incidents ("A high-speed chase four miles west of Seymour ended in a violent crash Friday … ."; Gillaspy, 1997) editorials ("At issue is what legal standards should be used in deciding whether a police officer's conduct was so unreasonable as to be unconstitutional … ."; unsigned editorial, 1997) a story about a citizens' group in Cincinnati that was protesting high-speed police chases; and, of course, the news feature or "in-depth piece" on high-speed chases, which is what we're really interested in. Every one of these stories, including the editorial and the longer feature, were legitimate examples of good journalism.

I've called this chapter "The News Peg" to get you thinking about features, backgrounders, enterprise stories and in-depth pieces, that can be prompted by simple news stories or even brief items that appear daily in the press or on TV.

At a minimum, including a news peg in your feature immediately answers the implicit question, "Why are we doing this story now?"

The following are types and examples of news pegs you can use to develop many features.

Anniversary Stories

Imagine today is December 7. What kind of features would you expect to see in the daily paper?

December 7, hmm? That's the anniversary of the Japanese attack on Pearl Harbor, which directly led to U.S. involvement in World War II.

Or, suppose today's date is November 22. It's become a cliché among people of a certain age in the United States to say, "Where were you on the day John F. Kennedy was assassinated?"

Either of these historic dates, and many others, could lead you to interview people about their memories of those times. Maybe they were direct participants (in the war, not the assassination, one would hope). Maybe a teacher recalls announcing to his or her class that the President has just been shot, then dismissing the students, or leading them to a hurry-up assembly in the auditorium. Such recollections could provide you with both the lead and the basis for stories people would read.

You would have to summarize the events—typically, individuals only remember history from their own, snail's eye point of view—so you might have to resort to some historical records or expert testimony. But you'd have to return to the real people whose lives were touched, or changed forever, by such important historical events.

What was life like on December 7, 1941, before Pearl Harbor changed everything? What was life like on November 22, 1963, before America lost its innocence, as some have liked to say? You could do a deep Sunday think piece: Did December 7, 1941, have to happen? If you read deeply enough into history, you'll find that the United States expected Japan to attack the Philippines first, and we were holding back our best ships in Hawaii in order to retaliate. We just didn't think the Japanese could strike that far from their shores. You'll also learn that U.S. radar picked up the attacking enemy aircraft, but the blips on the radar screen were ignored for hours, until it was too late. The anniversary of the attack on Pearl Harbor would be a good day to read about these things.

I don't want to push the war angle too far, but on February 15, 1998, many media outlets carried stories about the Spanish-American War, which dated from the sinking of the U.S. ship the *Maine* in Havana harbor 100 years earlier. There were no survivors from that date in history to interview, but I learned about the preexisting war hysteria in the United States, about the competition between Spain and the United States for domination in Latin America, and about Cuban rebels, who weren't much interested in either Spanish or U.S. domination. I wasn't looking to read up on the Spanish–American War when I woke up on the morning of February 15. But it was the 100th anniversary of the sinking of the *Maine*, and I couldn't avoid reading something about it in the morning paper because of the obvious news peg.

Medical Reports

You probably don't read too many medical journals, but newspapers routinely report on the latest issues of the *New England Journal of Medicine*, the *Journal of the American Medical Association*, and *Lancet* (a leading British medical journal). Newspapers also do stories prompted by the latest reports from the National Institutes of Health, Centers for Disease Control, and other governmental and nongovernmental health organizations.

I remember early reports about the first drug to slow the progress of the AIDS virus in humans. The drug, called AZT, is still around, but this was 1985 and I was working for a small newspaper in Champaign, Illinois. I remember the excitement of a fellow reporter who had just learned that a patient at a local hospital was taking AZT and that the patient and his doctors would talk on record about the experience.

The news peg was obvious. It wasn't just that AIDS was mushrooming in the national consciousness by then, but any "national" news story that had a "local" connection or angle automatically was news.

Many national medical stories—breast cancer, STDs, osteoporosis, and so on—often are reported by the major wire services, and these in turn often are localized. We interview local patients and local hospital spokespersons: Who is suffering locally, and what progress is being made locally to help the sufferers? Localizing breaking or national health news is the bread and butter of medical reporting in most small and midsize markets.

Anti-smoking and smoking-related disease stories have been big for a number of years now and will continue to be so for several years to come, I predict. As I am writing this chapter, the first lawsuit alleging death from secondhand smoke is being tried in Muncie, Indiana. Medical experts have long contended that second-hand smoke is hazardous; now a court will decide. Media from across the country are swarming around Muncie to cover the trial, which was by itself a news event. Yet many print media also are using the occasion of the highly publicized trial to talk about second-hand smoke in general, including interviewing other people who believe they have been adversely affected by it.

The Big Story

The smoking issue has generated thousands of stories in recent years, from business stories about how tobacco company stock prices might falter, to agricultural features on new uses for tobacco farmland in North Carolina or Kentucky, to features about "the patch" and nicotine chewing gum, to stories on how to curb teen smoking, to investigative reporting on tobacco company cover-ups and more. The issue of smoking has become such a big story, in other words, that anything tangentially related to it is by definition also a story. The big story, in other words, is a news peg for smaller stories, like a giant star in space that spits off enough gases to form new planets.

Trends

You've read the chapter on trend stories and how to do them by now. By definition, trends lead to new and diverse stories, or else they weren't real trends to begin with.

Let me explain. Throughout the mid- and late 1990s I was looking for women's sports stories to write about. I knew women's sports were a big story because of federal legislation dating back to the 1970s that mandated equal support for women's sports, but also because of the growing popularity of certain women athletes (Olympic speed skater Bonnie Blair, any number of professional women's tennis players, and so on). I did an award-winning story on girls' soccer in Indiana (that's what it was called—girls' soccer—so perhaps I'll be forgiven for using that term) when no one else in my department seemed interested in the topic. I put together two trends here. Soccer was gaining in popularity both nationally and in Indianapolis, and women's sports were continuing to pick up steam. Voilà, a story on girls' soccer in the state.

Another reporter I work with saw a local university's report on the growing number of Hispanics in Indianapolis. She immediately went out and profiled various members of the local Hispanic community, from the most educated and elite to those who came here as political refugees. She noted the reasons for the trend, but focused mostly on the faces and lives of the people involved. The news peg was news of the trend.

Crime reporting often has a news peg, too. Are crime statistics up in your community? It's likely you'll be assigned to interview residents of victimized neighborhoods and police officials on what's happening, and why. If there's been a particularly grizzly murder in your area, you may be asked to take a close look at the family of victim, and perhaps the family of the suspect. A sensational crime in itself can become the news peg for a host of associated stories. Later in this chapter you'll read part of a backgrounder from the *Savannah Morning News* pegged to the murder of a housewife who worked as a call girl for a local escort service.

Seasons

This may be the staple of features editors everywhere. By seasons, I mean any annual event. We have an Outdoors writer in Indianapolis who will visit the slopes in winter, the tulip poplar forests in fall, and do a story on wildflowers every spring (they bloom early, before the trees fully develop their leaves, because that's the wildflowers' only chance to catch the light, before the bigger trees overhead block out the light with their large leaves).

But we have Thanksgiving food stories and stories about entertaining over the Christmas holidays, Spring Break travel stories, fall football season preview stories, "What are the hottest Halloween costumes and masks this year?" stories, and so on.

Year in, year out, these stories break out of their cocoons like the ephemeral butterflies they are. One is reminded of the old injunction from the Biblical *Song of Songs*: "There is nothing new under the sun."

There are other examples of news pegs I could use, and I'll be suggesting how you can easily find more when we get to the exercises at the end of the chapter. But first, you'll read one full-text feature and two excerpts. Each was prompted by the following news events as they were reported in the late 1990s:

- Crash! I've picked a story from a Louisville newspaper to highlight the high-speed police chase problem in general. You'll read the full-text version here.
- JonBenet Ramsey: Dozens of newspapers ran full-length features and backgrounders on child beauty pageants after 6-year-old Ramsey was found bludgeoned to death in her Colorado home around Christmas 1996. The stories ranged from objective "what are child pageant"-type stories to highly charged exposés of the phenomenon. You'll read an excerpt of a story by Patricia Hagen of *The Indianapolis Star* pegged to the crime, even though Colorado is a long way from Indiana.
- The 1997 Savannah murder of a housewife who worked part-time as a call girl. The murder served as the peg for a feature on so-called escort services (excerpt only).

Here's the much heralded police chase story. It's a solid story, although my analysis that follows the text will point out a couple of shortcomings. (I think you learn as much from seeing problems exposed under the glare of a naked 100-watt bulb, as it were, as much as from reading stellar stories.) In any case, you'll easily be able to see here how a news event—a crash that resulted from a high-speed police chase—led to a worthwhile, in-depth follow-up story.

~.~~

Bystanders, Police Often Hurt: Dangerous chases spur police to look at policies and options*
by Kim Wessel

Late on the night of July 1, 1995, Edward L. Dudley went for a ride on his motorcycle. About the same time, Jeffersonville, Ind., police officer John Beury tried to stop Ricky G. White for a traffic violation and suspected driving under the influence.

White took off—the wrong way—south on Interstate 65, with Beury in pursuit. Eventually White's and Dudley's paths crossed—head on—in Louisville. Dudley was thrown from his motorcycle and injured so severely that he's had at least a dozen operations and has racked up $600,000 in medical bills. For the most part, he has to use a wheelchair to get around.

White pleaded guilty last month to a variety of charges—including trying to elude police. But still pending is a lawsuit in which Dudley, 34, and his wife, Connie, say that Jeffersonville and its police department are to blame for his injuries: If police hadn't chased White, the Dudleys contend, White wouldn't have run into him.

Such litigation—and concern about the killing and maiming of innocent third parties—have prompted police departments across the country to rethink their policies on pursuits, according to a report by the National Law Enforcement and Corrections Technology Center in Rockville, Md.

The dangers that chases pose to motorists and to police themselves also have given rise to new products designed to safely collar fleeing suspects.

The devices include relatively low-tech "Stop Sticks," which are placed on the road in front of a fleeing motorist to puncture the vehicle's tires. Louisville and Jefferson County police use them—as do both Indiana and Kentucky state police; the Jeffersonville Police Department does not.

But police may soon have in their arsenals more James Bond-like weapons, including the "Road Patriot," an automatically guided rocket-powered unit that emits an electromagnetic pulse that disrupts the vehicle's engine controls.

The need to put the brakes on high-speed chases—or find alternatives to them—is obvious to law-enforcement authorities: The most comprehensive federal study to date, the results of which were pub-

---

*From "Bystanders, Police Often Hurt: Dangerous chases spur police to look at policies and options" by K. Wessel. Copyright © 1996. *Courier-Journal & Louisville Times company.* Reprinted by permission.

lished in October, concluded that a collision can be expected in nearly a third of all pursuits. About 1 percent will result in a death.

While the suspect is usually the one who suffers—about 70 percent of the time injuries and deaths involved the occupants of the pursued vehicle—14 percent of the toll is on police and 15 percent on innocent bystanders.

As the national law-enforcement center puts it, because of the inherent risks, "There is no 'good' pursuit."

The Louisville Police Department allows pursuits only if an officer believes a suspect has committed a felony. The Jefferson County department's policy, which is less restrictive, says officers may pursue a suspect they believe has committed a felony, misdemeanor or other violation.

Jeffersonville had no policy in writing when Dudley was injured.

Police Chief Mike Pavey wouldn't comment on his department's role in that accident, or on the Dudleys' suit, which was filed in June in Jefferson Circuit Court, naming Beury, the department and the city of Jeffersonville as defendants.

Pavey said the department is writing a new policy, although he wouldn't say what it might include. But he said that if any chase "becomes too dangerous, it should be terminated."

Law-enforcement experts say it would be unwise to restrict pursuits too severely. If police don't chase suspects, there would be a greater incentive for them to flee, and go on to commit more crimes—and flee again.

In its model policy, the International Association of Chiefs of Police recommends that officers should pursue only those suspects they would have taken into custody. Officers should take into consideration the weather, their familiarity with the area and the threat to public safety, it says.

The Louisville department's policy says that "strong consideration" should be given to stopping a pursuit if the officer knows or has reason to believe that the suspect is intoxicated and poses an extreme safety hazard.

But police must consider if they let an obviously intoxicated suspect go and he proceeds to kill or injure someone, their department could still be liable.

It's a tough call, said Robert C. Crouse, the associate director of the Southern Police Institute at the University of Louisville.

"They're damned if they do and they're damned if they don't," he said. "They can be at fault for not doing anything just as much as they can be at fault for doing too much."

Crouse said Jeffersonville Officer Beury faced just such a vexing call: He had a suspect going the wrong way on an interstate and clearly posing a threat to public safety—whether he chased him or not.

"The officer is probably thinking, 'I cannot not do anything,'" Crouse said. "Myself, I wouldn't have had the guts to chase him."

(Beury drove in the emergency lane as he chased White south on northbound I–65.)

Crouse said police chases grow increasingly dangerous the longer they last. "The longer you keep the siren on, the more invincible you feel," Crouse said. "The adrenalin kicks in. In a long pursuit, you can get to the point at which you start to lose your best judgment."

For that reason, he said, some departments recommend that officers call off chases after a certain period of time, as short as seven minutes.

Until futuristic devices like the Road Patriot are widely available, officers themselves will have to decide whether to pursue.

In its report, the National Law Enforcement and Corrections Technology Center says: "The majority of research and professional literature has concluded that pursuit creates a far greater risk than benefit to the officer, the public and the suspect. The question is, 'Was it worth it?'"

Police officers must decide whether it's a greater danger to the public to pursue a suspect at high speed—or to let him go.

The news peg here is the anecdotal lead. The writer recreates a recent, tragic high-speed chase. I know the stretch of Interstate 65 she writes about quite well and can literally see the suspect's auto and the police cruiser crossing the Ohio River from Jeffersonville into Louisville.

It's a good news peg and anecdotal lead because this tragedy led to a lawsuit; you'll see that part of the problem is liability, not just innocent lives lost. In its simplest terms, liability means this: The defendant caused the problem, and damages were suffered. Prove those two things in court and you, the plaintiff, win. (Legal note: It doesn't matter in many states that you weren't the only person to cause the problem. The point is that if you, the defendant, didn't act the way you did, the outcome would have been different. Also, in the case given, the motorcyclist and his wife could have sued the reckless driver, Ricky White, who was going south on a northbound Interstate, but he's almost certainly "judgment-proof"; that is, he doesn't have any money, so you end up suing someone with deeper pockets.)

What "Bystanders, Police Often Hurt" accomplishes is to prove that there is a bigger issue behind the immediate headlines, and that officials are searching for answers. Also, it's very clear. The sentence structure is always no-nonsense, and one can tell that the reporter talked to a lot of experts. Having said that, it's a bit of a *"talking heads"* story; that is, we get some rather obvious quotes from officious-sounding but ultimately unhelpful expert sources.

Of course driving the wrong way on an Interstate highway at high speed is dangerous!

Also, had the story been longer, the author might have described one or two other tragic high-speed chases. These could have come after subheads in the story, which are those little chapter headings in boldface that separate sections of a longer story. As it is, only the lead is dramatic and visual, although the author certainly has collected some damning and interesting statistics.

In the writer's defense, we must acknowledge that the story really is hurt by the apparent refusal of every important actor in the crash itself to talk to the press!

The very last paragraph of " Bystanders, Police Often Hurt", too, is a bit gratuitous. It's the author interpreting or summing up the story for us. She doesn't have to do that. The quote in the next-to-last paragraph of the story had more punch to it, and most readers by then would have understood the dilemma that the author was trying to explain. Go back and re-read the next-to-last paragraph in the story. Do you really need the paragraph that follows it?

Overall, though, the story is fine. The news peg is clearly stated high up in the story, which should grab our attention (especially if we're Louisville readers), and the news peg helps us to understand why the author is pursuing the issue of such chases in the first place. The story clearly states the problem and touches on some technological solutions and policies that different police departments have vis à vis high-speed chases.

Here's the lead and nut graf for a story with a JonBenet Ramsey news peg written by Patricia Hagen of *The Indianapolis Star.*

> The murder of 6-year-old JonBenet Ramsey in Boulder, Colo., last month has put children's beauty pageants on trial. Pictures in magazines and on TV showing JonBenet competing in heavy makeup and feathered showgirl-type costumes have generated disgusted comments about the sexualization and abuse of children.
> Locally, contestants' mothers and pageant directors say they are horrified by the sex slaying, but they also maintain that pageants are getting a bad rap—unfairly. Pageants, they say, provide positive experiences for many children.

The news peg is very clear, reminding the reader of the recent murder that prompted the story, and the lead quite succinctly summarizes some of the thoughts and arguments sources will express in greater depth in the remainder of the story. Perhaps the key word in the above two paragraphs, though, is "locally," which instantly provides the transition from the national news event to hometown spokespersons.

Lots of other stories used the JonBenet Ramsey death as a news peg, sometimes with interesting twists. *The Baltimore Sun* (Kelley, 1997) looked at web sites and computer bulletin boards where amateur sleuths examined "evidence" and exchanged theories on "whodunnit." The *St. Louis Post-Dispatch* (Bosworth, 1997) interviewed several area pageant operators who lamented the fact that attendance was down in the wake of the Colorado murder. *The Washington Post* (O'Hanlon, 1997) took a lengthy look at the increased use of make-up by very young elementary school children, interviewing both children and their parents and teachers.

In each case, though, the stories were clearly pegged to the JonBenet Ramsey murder. It's as if the reporter was telling the reader, "This is why we're running this story now." In fact, helping explain why a story is in the paper on a given day is one of the prime functions of a clearly stated news peg up high.

Now, here's the feature lead and news peg from Ben Schmitt's story, "City's escort services; It's just companionship," written in the wake of a sensational call-girl murder in Savannah, GA, in 1997. The story appeared in the *Savannah Morning News*.

> Need a dinner companion or someone to show you around? Call an escort service.
> Want something more? The escort services say for the record that you should-n't waste your time calling.
> But 92-year-old Bertie Sharpe, who runs Rosie's Escort Service, offers this blunt assessment.
> "You want a girl, you call me and ask me if I have anybody available," Sharpe said. "I don't know what they do after that. I tell them whatever you do is y'all's business."
> Sharpe says she's been running escort services in Savannah for 65 years. For nearly that long, the services have come under fire as fronts for prostitution.
> One of the latest examples involved a 34-year-old Savannah woman who worked for an out-of-town service and was found beaten to death at a southside motel. No motive has been established.
> A suspect, Anthony Rodgers, was indicted recently by a Chatham County grand jury on murder charges involving the May 6 slaying of Phyllis Bennett.

Overall, the story is about escort services in Savannah, not about a particular murder. The paper had covered the murder and impending trial in its daily news pages; what Schmitt brought to the table was good background information on escort services generally (and historically) in this very touristy antebellum Southern town. The remainder of the story quotes escort service operators, police, and prosecutors, plus gives additional background on a prior criminal prosecution of an escort service prostitution ring.

ASSIGNMENT

Pick up a copy of your favorite daily newspaper. I don't care if it's *The Tribune* in Ames, Iowa (for you Iowa State students) or the *Chicago Tribune* (for you Northwestern or Northern Illinois students). Peruse the paper, especially the A section (typically the first section) and the Local section, for a news peg. Once you've found a suitable topic, go for it! Write a news feature prompted by that news peg.

For example, as I enter these words into my computer, I'm looking at *The* (Bloomington, Indiana) *Herald-Times* for August 25, 1997. "Drivers Reminded to Stop for School Buses," is the headline for a story on page 1. The news peg is the start of school; this date marks the first day of the first full week of classes in Bloomington public schools. It's a small feature, but it discusses school bus policies, parental concerns, and police insights regarding some pretty reckless drivers (Burck, 1997, p.1).

On page 3 of the same paper, I see a wire story about a policeman who was killed in Epsom, New Hampshire, (Rakowsky, MacQuarrie, 1997) after attending the funeral of two state troopers who had earlier been killed in the line of duty. It's a straight story following classic inverted pyramid lines, and not much more, but the whole macabre incident could serve as a news peg for more in-depth treatment of the dangers inherent in police work. The Bureau of Justice Statistics (a federal agency), the FBI, and any number of police associations and advocacy groups can give you plenty of sources to interview, as well plenty of numbers to use. Or, just start with your local police department. I'd call the story "Dangerous Duty."

ASSIGNMENT

As you go through your local paper (or a smaller paper from a surrounding community), look for items that seem to cry out for further treatment. Maybe you'll see an item about the first female kicker on the local high school football team as part of Friday night game coverage. Let's say she kicked a field goal and two Point After Touchdowns in the game. Her success could be the news peg for a personality profile, or a trend story on the increasing number of women in traditionally all-male sports. Or, you could do a story on problems the school now has providing dressing and restroom facilities for the young woman. These are just a few possibilities that might be prompted by one person's performance in one game. Your assignment is to find something as simple as the above, and to do a story.

Alternatively, get a calendar or book that features information such as, "On this date 25 years ago …," "On this date 50 years ago …," and so on. Look at a date about a month ahead of time and see if there's an anniversary of some important national event you could localize.

Real Feature Writing
Part II

5

The Focus Story

The continued popularity of *The Diary of Anne Frank* can be attributed, at least in part, to the successful way in which it identifies the murder of 6 million Jewish civilians in World War II to the experiences of one fairly interesting but ultimately ordinary young woman who was fated to die along with so many of her people. You can certainly find books about World War II or about the Holocaust that are filled with more facts and figures and names and dates and places and government documents and statistics and speeches and expert sources and so on, but because the focus was on a person not so very different than you or me, it makes it easier for us to relate to what happened in history.

That's the theory behind the *focus structure*. You take a complex issue—you'll be reading a *Miami Herald* story about the health care crisis later in this chapter—and reduce it in scope or scale to a manageable level, largely by reporting the story from the perspective of one person (or one family, or one community, as the case may be).

This technique can also be called the *microcosm/macrocosm approach*, in which you highlight the microcosm, or little picture, in an effort to better explain the macrocosm, or big picture. You probably know the origins of this technique best from the approach you learned in English class in middle school: Just give an example of what you mean to better illustrate your point.

Let's say you're doing a story on "living with AIDS." According to the 1998 Joint United Nations Programme on HIV/AIDS, more than 22 million people worldwide are living with AIDS, or acquired immunodeficiency syndrome (cited in Higgins, 1998). These victims all have a certain life expectancy; most have contracted the deadly AIDS virus in certain well-known ways; different therapies have had varying amounts of success and they all cost so many dollars a month to administer, and so on and so on. You could write a story that largely deals with all these facts and numbers, but who would read it? It would be a report, not a feature story.

Obviously, you're not going to focus on 22 million people, or even a fraction of that number. But you could focus on an individual, on one treatment center or group facility, or on the race for a cure at a single laboratory. This does not mean you ignore the larger story. Rather, you weave some of the basic facts (when AIDS was identified; how it gathered steam in the United States; how effective early efforts were to control its spread, and so on) and figures (the 22 million victims; life expectancy from the time one is first diagnosed; the cost of different anti-AIDS drugs, and so on) throughout your story. The big picture becomes a backdrop for the human drama you are revealing through your focus.

Look back in chapter 2 at either the story on midcareer teachers, or the story about Russian brides. To a certain extent, most trend stories can also be viewed as focus stories (or as microcosm/macrocosm stories, if you prefer that label). Why? Because the big picture is the trend itself, and the little picture is that person you choose to focus on, at least in your lead and ending, to illustrate the trend.

The story you're going to read here is, in spite of its irreverent title, a serious look at one of the greatest economic and social crises facing the United States today. It's a topic you've heard about but probably never really understood before. That's because the debate on health care reform has been controlled by economists, hospital administrators, and insurance executives, none of whom knows how to speak plain English or tell a story intelligibly.

~~~

Stayin' Alive: Ed Van Houten and America's Health-Care Dilemma*
by John Dorschner

At most, Ed Van Houten should have survived four years. Now it has been 10 and counting. The reason he's still alive is his wife, Marilyn. Everyone agrees on that.

Marilyn Van Houten is a nurse who works as a medical case manager; her specialty is dealing with hospitals and doctors on behalf of insurance organizations. She knows precisely how to fight the system, and she does—ferociously.

In her battles with the medical establishment, she has persuaded a half-dozen attorneys to help her out—at no cost to her. She has enlisted the support of social workers, government employees, the media, even congressmen. She wants her husband to have the very best care—regardless of the cost or who ultimately pays for it.

* From "Stayin' Alive: Ed Van Houten and America's Health-Care Dilemma" by J. Dorschner. Copyright © 1991, *The Miami Herald*. Reprinted by permission.

So far, hospitals have been footing most of the bills. For the past two years, Ed Van Houten has not spent a night at home. His room at Miami's Baptist Hospital is $354 a day. His high-tech air bed, to protect against bed sores, costs an additional $155 a day. His Pampers diapers cost $3.75 each. Every time he gets feverish and needs a bag of ice, it's $15. He has a $20,000 artificial hand he hasn't used in months.

He has excellent insurance: He's covered by both Medicare and private insurance. But his medical bills are so enormous that he is doing something many people consider impossible—running out of Medicare coverage. And even though he is obviously catastrophically ill, his insurers have frequently refused to pay for his treatment, claiming it is not medically necessary for him to be in a hospital. In his nine months at Baptist, the hospital has yet to receive a cent on his outstanding bill: $350,000 at last count.

That's obviously tough on the hospital. But it is also hard on people who use hospitals and on those who buy insurance to pay for hospitalization. Ed is part of the reason that his bag of ice costs $15. Cases like his have helped push hospital costs and health insurance premiums into the stratosphere.

Several times, hospitals have tried to get rid of him. One hospital notified him he was trespassing; a uniformed officer walked into his room and formally evicted him. His nine months at Baptist means he has been there far longer than any other patient in the 500-bed facility. Several times, Baptist has tried to get him to leave. Marilyn has adamantly objected. Taking Ed out of the hospital, she believes, would kill him.

"His quality of life is terrible," she says. "I think it stinks. But he wants to stay alive, and I support him in that. How do you let a 45-year-old person just die? So I'm doing all I can."

Of course, no matter how many thousands of dollars of care are lavished on her husband, his is a hopeless case. Many people would prefer death to the myriad ills that steadily consume what is left of Ed's life.

"On a scale of 1 to 10," Ed says, "the quality of my life is about point 5."

When he is alert, his one pastime is watching television. His favorite show is "Highway to Heaven," a midafternoon series of reruns about an angel who, to make up for the sins of his corporeal existence, returns to Earth to do good deeds for common folk.

Ed is often grumpy. Nasty, even. Frequently, he explodes in anger at nurses and doctors. He often refuses medication or tests. Nurses tend to dislike him. His doctors describe him with words like "difficult" and "manipulative."

Much of the time, he lies in bed with the curtains drawn, the television off, wearing only an adult-size paper diaper. He is missing his left hand. He is blind in one eye, deaf in one ear. His kidneys don't work. He suffers from heart disease and a rare lung disease that is usually found only in black women. He is a diabetic. His bones are so brittle that a recent coughing fit broke his hip. He has high blood pressure. His gallbladder has been removed. So has his parathyroid gland.

He suffers from horrendous acne—black spots littering his back, which cause intense itching that he can't scratch. He has calcium deposits that cause odd lumps on his hands, arms and back. He suffers from a brain disorder of uncertain origin. Often, he is in a "fog," and weeks go by without his being conscious of anything.

He suffers from depression and sometimes contemplates suicide, though his wife says he doesn't want to die. Dying would be easy: All he would need do is demand that nurses stop hooking him up to the dialysis machine that three times a week cleans the wastes from his blood—the machine that has kept him alive for the past 10 years.

Some would say that's long enough.

A brutal question: Should Ed Van Houten be allowed to live?

Health-care experts are beginning to wonder: Is it time to put strict limits on medical care? Is it worth hundreds of thousands of dollars a year to keep someone like Ed Van Houten alive?

While Ed soaks up enormous amounts of medical services, millions of poor people can't afford even basic medical treatment. Is it worth it to keep Ed alive when, say, a hundred destitute women with breast cancer could be treated for the same amount of money? Or perhaps a thousand impoverished pregnant women could be given crucial prenatal care?

"This is a very important case," says Dr. Raul De Valasco, Ed's primary physician, "because it deals with the main issues: The question is, who decides and who pays?"

He means who decides who can receive lifesaving technology. In our society, that's the easy part. Theoretically, in the United States—at least for now—everyone is entitled to have his or her life saved by medicine. The dying man with a bullet in his brain will get tens of thousands of dollars in treatment in an emergency room—even though there's not a 1-in-10,000 chance he will survive. A premature baby weighing a few ounces will receive equally expensive care, even though chances are that, if the baby does survive, he or she will be brain-damaged.

The question of who pays is much more difficult, for no one really wants to pay for the care of people like Ed Van Houten.

Stephen Sapp, a specialist in medical ethics at the University of Miami: "How much is a human life worth? Can we put a dollar value on human life, and if we do, who's going to pay for it? How much right does the individual have to demand from society unlimited health-care resources, when there is such a crying need in so many other areas if society?"

Ed Van Houten was born and reared in Homestead, Fla. His father was an internal auditor for the county. His mother was a telephone operator and a diabetic. When he was 15, he learned he had juvenile diabetes. He didn't think much about it at the time, but he hated the rigid diet restrictions that limited his intake of anything sugary—from ice cream to beer. Like many juvenile diabetics, he occasionally rebelled and went off the diet.

In 1969, when his mother was 45, her kidneys began failing. At the time, scientists were working on an artificial kidney machine, and a few units were scattered around the country, including one at Jackson Memorial Hospital in Miami. Tens of thousands were clamoring for the $600-a-week treatment. Hospitals set up what became known as "God committees"—panels that would decide who would live by going on dialysis, and who would die.

Ed's mother didn't make the cut. As a diabetic, she had too many complications. A few days after her kidneys failed, she slipped into a coma and died.

Dr. J. Phillip Pennell, a dialysis expert, was a member of these early "God committees." Not coincidentally, he now teaches ethics to medical students at the University of Miami. "They were tough decisions. I've sent home 28-year-old mothers of three to die," he says. In her case, there just weren't any machines available.

Nobody in the United States wanted to make such nasty decisions. No one wanted to send people home to die. But no one wanted to pay to keep them alive either. "Dialysis is expensive treatment," says De Velasco, an affluent doctor. "Not even someone like me could afford to pay for it out of my own pocket."

Only one entity had a deep enough pocket: The federal government. In the early '70s the medical establishment—and desperate patients with failing kidneys—persuaded Congress to expand Medicare, which had been intended for the elderly, to include dialysis patients, regardless of their ages. Today 116,000 Americans are kept alive by dialysis, costing Medicare $2.7 billion a year for just the basic, thrice-weekly treatments.

At the time of the legislation, Ed Van Houten wasn't paying much attention. His kidneys were working fine. He attended Miami-Dade Community College for two years, then bounced around the country as a jack of all trades. He returned to south Florida and went to work for a fence company. In 1974 he was sent to a home to give an estimate to a young divorced nurse, Marilyn Goonen, who had a 2-year-old child. He asked her out. They dated for several years before getting married.

In 1981, while working in Metro-Dade's Building and Zoning Department, Ed suffered a mild heart attack. The hospital ran tests. "I have bad news for you," his doctor said. Because of his diabetes, his kidneys were failing.

Before he could feel much panic, his doctor assured him that dialysis machines could keep him alive for a long time.

For the first year, Ed's insurance paid about 80 percent of the cost. That still left the Van Houtens owing thousands. Doctor bills were mounting. The Van Houtens watched the bills roll in. They couldn't afford to pay them. Some people might have made at least token payments—a few dollars a month—but Marilyn didn't see any point to that. "They were getting thousands, probably tens of thousands, from the insurance, and I don't think they were expecting us to pay anything."

Ed hoped for a kidney transplant, but doctors preferred more stable, healthier candidates. Ed had "brittle diabetes," an uncommonly severe form of the disease: His blood-sugar levels fluctuated wildly, sometimes soaring up, threatening heart attacks, and sometimes plummeting, threatening comas. He was particularly vulnerable to infections and broken bones. His history of dialysis-related transfusions had left his blood filled with antibodies that, surgeons felt, were likely to reject a new organ.

In 1982, after two years of dialysis, Ed began having trouble walking. He frequently felt weak and dizzy. At age 37, he retired. His pension was $415 a month, but virtually all of it—about $405—went to maintain a work-related health insurance policy with Metropolitan. Marilyn was convinced they were going to need all the insurance they could get.

For several years, Ed did quite well. He went on fishing trips with his stepson and once even traveled to Jamaica. Then, in August 1988, leaving a poker game at a friend's house, he stumbled on a step and scraped his legs. The wounds became infected, and that threw his metabolism out of whack. His blood sugar plummeted, his calcium level soared. He went into a coma.

Following standard procedures, nurses used loose restraints to tie his hands to the bed railings so he wouldn't accidentally disconnect the IVs and monitor wires. Marilyn worried about what the restraints would do to his poor circulation, but Ed was so ill that the nurses considered it an irrelevant side issue. After a week, to the surprise of his doctors, Ed emerged from the coma. A few days later, he returned home, Marilyn noticed that the little finger on his left hand was darkening almost to black: It was dying. A month later, at Doctors' Hospital, the finger was amputated.

"It was painless," said Ed. "So I went home. At the end of a week, I started to get pain again in my hand. I pushed down and an infection came out of the bandage."

He was admitted immediately to Jackson. The hand had to come off.

"I didn't have general anesthesia," Ed said. "It was a local. I could hear the saw. And I could feel it. They said I couldn't feel anything, but I could. They make you a little woozy, that's all." After the operation, he went into another coma.

It was sometime during Ed's stay at Jackson that a resident physician asked Marilyn: "You want me to write a 'no code' for you?"

Marilyn understood: "No code" meant that no extraordinary measures would be used to keep Ed alive.

"Obviously," the resident told her, "he has nothing to live for."

Marilyn had been one of the first staff members of Miami Hospice back in the '70s. She had spent several years helping terminally ill patients die peacefully, with dignity, without all the high-tech machines of modern medicine that can prolong life—and pain. But now, hearing this opinion from the resident, she rebelled. She simply couldn't stand the thought of her husband slipping off during a medical crisis. Ed wasn't terminal. He didn't want to die. He had been through too many painful experiences to give up now.

Once again, Ed pulled out of the coma. Jackson doctors announced he was fit to be discharged. Marilyn knew she couldn't take him home. He was too sick for that, and his insurers didn't pay for home-care nurses. Panicked, Marilyn decided perhaps "rehab" was the answer.

In a rehabilitation unit of a hospital, Ed could get physical therapy. Without therapy, the muscles of his limbs would atrophy. With therapy, he might be able to climb from a bed into a wheelchair. But rehab was also a way to keep Ed in the hospital and circumvent Medicare restrictions.

Under Medicare, hospitals and doctors for years had arranged treatments and charged prices that the federal government had paid for without question. Medicare costs soared. In the early '80s, when Medicare costs were zooming up by 19 percent a year—almost five times the rate of inflation—the federal government decided it had enough. Medicare fixed reimbursements. Removing a gallbladder, mending a broken hip—each procedure had a price tag. No more blank checks.

There was one exception: rehabilitation. Because the amount of time required for rehab varied greatly among patients, Medicare basically still paid what the hospitals charged.

To medical economists, this was a loophole. To Marilyn, it was an opportunity. Using the contacts she knew from her work as a case manager, she found a place that was willing to accept her husband. On Sept. 9, 1989, Ed entered the rehab unit at South Miami Hospital.

The therapy began, but much of the time, Ed was too exhausted to do the exercises. Sometimes, he blew up at the therapists and told them to go away. To justify the Medicare charges, the hospital had to show Ed was making progress. But Ed was not progressing. The hospital insisted he leave.

Marilyn began calling her contacts. Palmetto Health Center, a nursing home, agreed to take him. Marilyn didn't trust nursing homes. She saw them as places for people to linger for a bit before they died—warehouses for the elderly. Most nursing-home care was handled by aides who weren't skilled nurses: Marilyn didn't believe they could deal with Ed's blood-sugar crises—any one of which could lead to coma and death. But she took him to the Palmetto nursing home anyway. She felt she had no choice.

On Dec. 12, 1989, Marilyn was almost relieved when a severe ear infection got Ed readmitted to South Miami Hospital. The ear infection proved resistant to antibiotics. For a while, doctors wondered if the infection had spread to his brain.

"This," said Ed, "is where the real fun begins."

If a patient is stoic and sadly adorable, nurses flock to his care. A 9-year-old poster child can be irresistible. But in real life, sick people are often grumpy and spiteful—angry at their illness, angry at their dependence on machines and caregivers. At South Miami, Ed was an exceptionally angry, argumentative and hostile patient.

Sometimes he refused to take insulin. Sometimes he refused to allow his blood pressure to be taken. He yelled at nurses. He yelled at doctors. He got angry at the incessant "finger sticks," pricks of blood they used to measure his blood sugar, because he had only one hand it was constantly sore from the pricks. He was, concedes Marilyn, "a nightmare patient."

Dr. Ray Lopez, a neurologist, was called in. He decided that Ed was suffering from metabolic encephalopathy, a brain disorder probably caused by chemical imbalances in the blood. The effects could be anything from mild confusion—the "fog" that Ed often found himself in—to a coma. If Ed was alert, Lopez reported, the encephalopathy could reduce natural inhibitions, causing him to lash out in anger.

Of course, Ed was more than unpopular. He was a major financial liability. Many hospital administrators claim Medicare now pays only about half the average patient's bill. For unusually complicated cases, it pays even less. Medicare has provisions for complications, but they're not huge. Ed's case has extraordinary complications because he usually is fighting many ailments at the same time.

At South Miami Hospital, Ed's bill ran up to $180,000. Out of this, his insurance paid only $44,500.

On Jan. 12, 1990, a South Miami Hospital committee reviewed Ed's case and notified him that his stay there was no longer medically necessary. This news was communicated in a formal document that also stated Medicare was denying a further payment for his stay.

Ed's doctor's agreed he was stable enough to leave the hospital. Marilyn appealed the decision to an outside Medicare arbitrator, but the arbitrator ruled in the hospital's favor, at which point, Marilyn developed a simple strategy: She and Ed refused to leave.

The hospital responded with social workers who recommended nursing homes, particularly a facility in nearby Kendall, Fla., called Green Briar, which described itself as a "rehabilitation and comprehensive care center."

Green Briar costs roughly $360 a day—about 40 percent of what a hospital costs. To Medicare, that's a big savings. Marilyn's attitude is you get what you pay for. To her, Green Briar was just another nursing home. She was convinced Ed wouldn't survive it.

In early February 1990, after considerable debate, South Miami Hospital took an extraordinary step: It moved to evict Ed Van Houten. Marilyn was astounded. "I didn't believe a hospital would do such a thing," she said.

Marilyn called all the television stations, hoping that publicity would force the hospital to change its mind. When eviction day came, only one TV crew showed up, but that was enough to get the hospital to back down.

Two days later, however, a hospital security guard and an ambulance crew entered Ed's hospital room and, within minutes, slid Ed onto a gurney and wheeled him out.

When told their destination was Green Briar, Marilyn insisted on being taken to the nearest hospital emergency room. The ambulance delivered Ed to Baptist Hospital, where officials decided that if he was medically stable enough to leave South Miami Hospital, there was no reason he should be admitted to Baptist.

But Marilyn and Ed refused to leave the emergency room. Shortly after dawn, a hospital social worker showed up and once again tried to persuade Marilyn to take Ed to Green Briar. Exhausted after the long night, Ed in a fog beside her, Marilyn gave in. An ambulance took them to the nursing home.

During Ed's first three weeks at Green Briar, Marilyn was terrified something would happen. It did. It began with Ed's complaining of chest pain.

After several hours of uncertainty, Marilyn finally got him taken back to the Baptist emergency room. His blood sugar was more than five times higher than normal. "A doctor told me, 'My God, I've never seen a blood sugar that high.'" Marilyn says, "A little later, his tongue started protruding. I yelled for the nurse. He was in V-Tac." This means his heart was fluttering out of control. Ed was rushed into the coronary care unit.

Marilyn believes this incident proves she is right about the differences between nursing homes and hospitals: The nursing home staff hadn't been able to keep up with Ed's condition. "His potassium was way up. His blood sugar was way up. None of that need have happened."

Russell Silverman, the administrator at Green Briar, thinks Green Briar did a fine job. "Altogether, he was with us for three months, and only once did he need to be hospitalized. This was a patient with unstable conditions, and yet almost all the time, we were able to handle him. I think that proves Green Briar was the right facility for him."

In fact, Ed's blood sugars have sometimes gotten wildly out of control even when he's been in a hospital. The difference is that, in a hospital, the emergency-intensive care equipment is right there, for immediate use. For Marilyn, Silverman's "only once" is a gross over-simplification: "Only once" could mean Ed's death.

After Ed had been in Baptist six days, Marilyn dropped by his room after work to find him gone. A nurse told her he had been transferred back to Green Briar. He had been in a "fog" and hadn't objected.

Marilyn suspected that Baptist had shipped Ed out while she wasn't around so it could unload a very expensive patient: Ed had run up $165,000 in bills in his Baptist stays up to that point. Insurance paid for only a tenth of that.

Ed spent two more months at the nursing home without a crisis. Finally, Marilyn persuaded Sunrise Rehabilitation Hospital in neighboring Broward County to take him. It was 40 miles from home, and it wasn't a full-care hospital, but as far as Marilyn was concerned, it was better than a nursing home.

Sunrise was expensive, even by hospital standards—$325 a day for the room, $299 a day for a bed similar to the one he'd had for half that amount at Baptist (a bed he could have bought for $6,000 wholesale, $10,000 retail), plus miscellaneous expenses. Altogether, Sunrise's charges were running more than $2,100 a day. What's more, Medicare refused to pay the Sunrise bill: Once again, the feds said that Ed's stay at the hospital was medically unnecessary.

On July 20 Sunrise told Ed he should leave. He was given a letter, stating that he was personally responsible for the bill. It is a fascinating document: "The total amount due, charges plus deposit, is $211,347.50. Please make your check payable to Sunrise Rehabilitation Hospital and remit immediately."

Marilyn saw the bill and laughed. Collection agencies called her at all hours at home; some even had her beeper number. They sent earnest letters. "Is there any reason for further delay? As you know, Mr. Van Houten, a good payment record is important. Consequently, you should make immediate efforts for settlement."

Marilyn hated to iron, so she used the ironing board as the table for medical bills. It was covered with stacks of paper. Even now, she has no idea how much money they owe. The total indebtedness has become irrelevant: If any of the hospitals or doctors took them to court, the Van Houtens would be forced into bankruptcy.

"These figures," she says, "are so far beyond my comprehension, I don't even think about them."

Marilyn doesn't have time to think about much of anything. She earns $29,000 a year from her main job, doing medical liaison work for a group of self-insured construction companies. She scrambles to make ends meet by having two part-time jobs. The jobs require considerable travel, and she rushes from appointment to appointment throughout southern Florida. Her car is a 1988 Chrysler LeBaron with 66,000 miles on it. She recently spent $400 for repairs on it and wonders how long she can keep it going. When she can, she tries to spend a little time with her son, who's now 18. Her routine she describes in a single word: "chaotic."

For a month, Ed refused to leave Sunrise. Then he developed a severe infection: an irrefutable medical reason for hospitalization. Sunrise, which specialized in rehab, wasn't equipped to handle the infection. On Thursday, Aug. 16, 1990, an ambulance carried Ed once again to Baptist, where he was admitted.

He has gone through a dozen serious infections. Several times, he has been in intensive care. After his 10th visit to the operating room, the nurses joked he was a "regular commuter." But between crises, there have been times when the hospital staff thought he was well enough to be discharged. Of the first 180 days he was at Baptist, administrators estimate that only 55 were defined in Medicare terms as being "medically necessary."

"They'd tell me," Marilyn says, "'He's going to Green Briar.' For most people, that'd be the end of it. They don't understand the system. I'd say, 'No, he's not.' And that really stops them. They're not used to people disagreeing with them."

Still, Marilyn was running out of options. Medicare allows only 90 hospital days and 100 nursing home days "per benefit period." That means per illness. The only way a patient can start a new "benefit period" is to spend 60 consecutive days at home. The regulations had been written to limit huge costs of caring for patients like Ed Van Houten.

What Marilyn and Ed really wanted was to work out a deal so the insurers would pay for his care at home, with round-the-clock aides. Ed felt he would be comfortable there, and he wouldn't be forgotten like he might be in a nursing home. What's more, the care wouldn't be nearly as expensive as it would in a hospital.

The problem was that neither Medicare nor Metropolitan, the secondary policy, had provisions for home care. Still, Marilyn occasionally met with an attorney, hoping that some legal muscle might do some good. She had a vague idea that if Ed's Medicare benefits were exhausted, Metropolitan would become the primary insurer. Medicare never alters its rules, but perhaps Metropolitan executives would go "out of policy" and realize home care would be the best solution.

"It's one of those things," Marilyn said one day when she was exhausted, "that makes so much sense that no one wants to do it."

In December Baptist's administrators met with Marilyn and Ed's doctors. To overcome her objections to Green Briar, the hospital volunteered to do his blood work so he could have quick, accurate readings. It said it would also provide for three ambulance trips a week to the dialysis center.

But even that didn't reassure Marilyn. Ed had only about two weeks of nursing home days left under Medicare. After that, the only alternative would be to go on Medicaid, the federally supported program for the poor. Medicaid pays no more than $95 a day for nursing-home care, and a facility like Green Briar—which can receive more than $400 a day from Medicare for its complicated patients such as Ed—refuses to accept Medicaid patients. So even if Ed had wanted to go there, he couldn't afford to.

At the meeting, Green Briar officials insisted that Marilyn sign papers promising that she personally would be responsible for his bills. She refused.

Minor crises—each of which would be a rare and major event for most other people—came and went. In late January Ed started suffering such excruciating pain that he decided he wanted to die. He told Marilyn of his decision by phone.

She was calm. "If that's how you feel, I'll understand," she said. But as soon as she hung up, she called Al and Chris Horton, two charismatic Catholics who often pray with Ed at the hospital. Crying, Marilyn told them what Ed was proposing. Al Horton raced over to the hospital. He told Ed that such a momentous decision should be left in God's hands, not man's.

"Al's and Chris' argument is He keeps saving me, so there must be a reason," Ed says. "They keep telling me what an example I am for other people. Only God knows the pain I have been through—mentally and physically. And I'm sure He doesn't want me to suffer, but He keeps bringing me back, so there has to be a reason. Al kept at me and kept at me. Marilyn broke down and cried. So I kind of gave in."

Ed went to dialysis. Later, X-rays discovered the reason for his pain: He had a broken hip. His bones had become so brittle that a coughing fit had caused the fracture.

In some European countries, such as Britain, faceless government committees have set stringent requirements for patients applying for dialysis. They're much more likely to reject applications or set arbitrary cutoffs. In some places, anyone over 55 can't begin dialysis. You are 56, your kidneys fail, you die. Sorry.

In the United States, such excruciating decisions are avoided. The only exception is in Oregon, where the legislature had created state health insurance that would include all those who are not now insured, including 120,000 not covered by Medicaid, plus employees of small companies and high-risk patients.

But there's a catch. The state will cover more people by covering fewer ailments. A committee of health experts has developed a 714-item list of medical problems. Treatment for ailments at the top of the list—tuberculosis, pneumonia, appendicitis—can yield great medical benefit at relatively little cost. Treatment for those at the bottom of the list—AIDS cases in which patients are likely to die within five years, terminal cancer cases, premature babies born weighing under 1.3 pounds—is unlikely to produce significant medical improvement and costs a great deal. So the extreme preemies and the AIDS patients will be allowed to die.

Mark Gibson, a legislative aide, says that did not mean these patients would be abandoned: "They will get comfort care, with pain medications, at home or in a hospice. But we won't be spending huge amounts on them."

Marilyn understands the Oregon theory, but she's nervous about its execution: "I know there has to be some sort of restraint put on spending. I know there are indigents who need health care, and I feel real bad for them, but I don't see why Ed shouldn't get care just because there are indigents. How can you decide that someone shouldn't have health care? I can't see someone saying, 'He can't have dialysis because he doesn't have an arm and he's not a useful member of society.' That's the kind of thing the Nazis used to do. Who knows what kind of criteria might be used?"

Ed: "I basically believe each individual has the right to preserve his life if he should wish to continue. I know my care has been expensive, but then you look around at all the waste. The Air Force spends $2,500 for a hammer. The Defense Department spends billions of dollars for weapons that don't get used. So you talk about a $300,000 medical bill, that's like a drop in the bucket. I don't feel like I'm ripping anybody off."

Medicare generally refuses to pay any bills until a patient is discharged from the hospital. The federal bureaucracy's requirements—and Ed's complications—are so extraordinary that even Baptist's experts can't figure out if Medicare will pay anything at all.

It's possible that Medicare will decide Ed has exhausted his benefits. If it does, Baptist hopes to collect from Metropolitan, Ed's second insurer. Again, the hospital's experts are in uncharted territory. One inkling of how complex the situation is: Metropolitan has demanded to see copies of Ed's medical records for the past eight months. These records are so voluminous that Baptist is asking Metropolitan to pay for photocopying them. The price: $5,000.

Pennell, the medical ethics specialist at the University of Miami, says Ed's $350,000-plus bill at Baptist is somewhat misleading. The only real cost to the hospital, Pennell points out, is for the services and supplies he consumes. Once the hospital has bought a high-tech air bed, it doesn't really cost hundreds a day to use it. Of the hundreds of thousands Ed was charged, only a small portion was an actual cash expense. "It's a paper loss," says Pennell, "a potential loss of income."

But that doesn't mean Baptist is padding the bill. The non-profit hospital's charges are relatively cheap compared with those of other area hospitals. Baptist really needs hundreds of thousands of dollars from patients like Ed to keep the hospital running, and if it can't get the money from Ed, then it needs to get it from other patients.

One recent afternoon, Ed turned off the TV and did a little talking. "I'm feeling pretty good," he said. "For the moment. Of course," he said, chuckling weakly, "for me, good is with an asterisk."

Epilogue

After a year and a day in Miami's Baptist Hospital, after running up a bill of $470,000 that no one wanted to pay, after heated battles with administrators who wished to ship him off to a nursing home, Ed Van Houten decided he should leave in style.

In August, on his last night there, he gave a party in his hospital room for nurses and friends. Everyone was ecstatic: Ed Van Houten was getting what he had always wanted: round-the-clock care in his own home. Later that night, as ambulance attendants wheeled him into his suburban Miami home, he shouted: "Thank you, God."

Two weeks earlier, the Van Houtens were informed that, despite what insurers had steadfastly claimed, home care was now possible. In early August, Metro-Dade, the county government that had been Ed's employer, entered the picture. Metro-Dade had been self-insured, with Metropolitan administering the policy. Metro-Dade administrators decided that eventually they would be paying Ed's bill at Baptist Hospital because his Medicare funding had run out. "When we figured out it was our baby," a Metro-Dade official said, "we decided to take a very aggressive posture."

A special case manager determined it would cost $13,000 a month to treat Ed at home compared to $39,000 a month in the hospital. Although home care was not covered by Ed's insurance policy, Metro-Dade decided it was the best solution.

On his first full day home, surrounded by his friends and his dogs, Ed was filled with hope. He even was planning to start a job, using the telephone to organize sales that would bring contributions to the Catholic Archdiocese of Miami.

"It's really amazing," he said, "how things can turn out."

Still, Marilyn worries. She figures within a year or two, they will have used up Ed's $1 million lifetime reserve with Metropolitan. "It will be interesting to see," she says thoughtfully, "what happens next."

Here's a fun assignment for extra credit: Add up all the dollar amounts quoted for various expenses and services in this story. I think it's safe to say you have never read a story about any economic issue with as many numbers as snowflakes in a North Dakota blizzard.

Yet "Stayin' Alive" was a compelling read. The doggedness of Marilyn Van Houten was transparent. Ed's personality was pretty clear, too, and not always likable.

But the numbers, the deadening weight and sheer magnitude of the costs and expenses and complications with who would pay for what, was brought home brilliantly by the writer. The execution of this story, like that of a successful military campaign, was brilliant, and John Dorschner made the perfect call when he decided to use a focus structure for this story. I think everyone who reads this story can understand the health care crisis in the United States because it was shown via one case study in south Florida.

Now, before I go into a more detailed analysis of this story, note the overall structure or organization:

> *The Lead*—The sad predicament of Ed Van Houten and his embattled wife, Marilyn, followed by what is a really a synopsis or abstract of most of the story to come. It's not really an "anecdotal" lead, although often that's just what you'll want in a focus story.
>
> *The Nut Graf and Transition*—The author sums up the dilemma of rising health care costs in the paragraph that starts, "Health-care experts are beginning to wonder: Is it time to put strict limits on medical care?" Note also the line in the 22nd paragraph that reads, " … for no one really wants to pay for the care of people like Ed Van Houten." That one line is the transition; it tells you the story is going to be as much about "people like Ed Van Houten" as about Ed himself.
>
> *The Body*—Where the author details chronologically the process by which Ed Van Houten was bumped from one facility to another as his wife fought to save him, and also where we learn some nice biographical background about both Van Houtens.
>
> *Ending*—Not hard to find in this story. Dorschner relies on one of the oldest literary devices in the book: He gives us an epilogue, or the story after the story. It's really a climax to the story of Ed Van Houten (for now, at least), and the author is following a storytelling technique by delivering the climax at the end of the article, where it belongs.

Now for the details. If you made a list of sources for this story it would look like a list from almost any health care crisis story: a medical ethicist; a nursing home administrator; an insurance spokesman; the patient's primary physician. There is nothing surprising about including any of these sources in this story. But the sources don't predominate. The narrator in this story always is John Dorschner; we are not plagued by a bunch of talking heads whom we do not know.

There is a fine use of quotes here, as well. Remember, if the source can say it better than you, or the quote reveals some of the source's personality, then by all means quote the source. Dorschner does this effectively in the unflattering quote attributed to Marilyn Van Houten ignoring her husband's doctor, hospital, and nursing home bills: "They were getting thousands, probably tens of thousands, from the insurance, and I don't think they were expecting us to pay anything."

She is committed to helping her husband, which is wonderful, but I learned from that one quote that I wouldn't want to take a personal check from the lady! Quoting Marilyn is much more effective than simply stating that she doesn't think she has an obligation to pay for her husband's health care.

Consider, too, the story"s "pull the plug" issue, the issue of letting someone die because it's too implausible or expensive to keep him or her alive: The author doesn't begin the paragraph by saying, *One of the greatest challenges facing Marilyn Van Houten in her heroic struggle to keep her desperately ill husband alive was when she was confronted with the issue of choosing to let her husband die rather than insisting that every weapon in the high-tech medical arsenal be employed to save him.*

Dorschner could have written that, but he uses a simple quote (part of a dialogue between two sources in the story, not a quote in the form of an answer to one of Dorschner's questions) instead. It's when we read of the time a doctor said to Marilyn: "You want me to write a 'no code' for you?"

We get the message.

So, quotes are used very effectively in this story. They're used sparingly, too. You don't find that many quotes in this long story. (Try adding them up.)

And the dollar amounts and other figures: Obviously, we need to know what Ed's total bill ran to, and what the limits of Medicare benefits are, as well as why a bag of ice costs $15. Any writer could have included these details in his or her story, but most would have bogged down under the sheer volume of numbers.

Dorschner succeeds in presenting the complicated math because he never forgets that he's telling a "story" first. Why is Medicare nearly bankrupt? Dorschner could have given us a treatise on this subject, but instead we are introduced to one key reason—expensive dialysis treatments—in the context of Ed's reliance on dialysis machines. The problem is that Medicare has to pay for so many people like Ed, and it adds up. It is also at this point in the story that we learn how in England, for example, the government just won't pay for elderly people who need the treatment, meaning they're allowed to die. You see the human drama, the accountant's red ink, and the ethical issues all in one.

Why does an air bed cost $299 a day, especially when you could buy the darn thing for $6,000? Dorschner also puts those numbers in context.

As with all those numbers, expert sources intrude in the story only when they are relevant to the development of the narrative. Ed almost dies at Green Briar? Then, and only then, will we hear from a spokesman for Green Briar.

Ed is suffering from metabolic encephalopathy, among other terrible conditions? You are not going to read an article about metabolic encephalopathy unless you're a 4th-year pre-med student. But we've read about this constant "fog" that Ed is in, and it is in the context of trying to understand the "fog," which seems both interesting and depressing, that we are willing to read about a plausible medical explanation for it.

Try this informal exercise: Draw a timeline of Ed Van Houten's illness and stays at different health care facilities. "Stayin' Alive" is essentially chronological in development, so this should be easy.

Now, fill in places where expert sources are quoted on some of the real issues in this story, as well as places where some of the stunning costs and numbers are revealed. In all cases, except perhaps for the lead and nut graf, the writer puts the drama and story ahead of the numbers and talking head experts.

Here's another little experiment: Comb through the story and see if you can find many obscure, high-falootin' words or vocabulary that would tend to show off what an educated and fine writer John Dorschner is. There are a few medical and accounting terms that he defines for us (defining complex terms is always an excellent idea), but other than that, the writing in this story is very plain. We have nouns and verbs, but not so many adjectives and adverbs, which often are signs of overwriting. The writing here is powerful in large measure because it is so direct and brutal (can you hear Ed's hand being sawed off? Can you see his acne)? I want you to think about that, especially those among you who believe every feature story should be the literary event of the season.

Another thing I like about this story is that it's evenhanded. One can easily imagine an advocate for health care and health insurance reform writing a story based on Ed and Marilyn. But it most likely would have been laced with hash judgments against the cruel hospital administrators who wanted to throw Ed in the street, while dripping with compassion for the poor, desperate, innocent victims known as Ed and Marilyn Van Houten. Such a heavy-handed treatment would have led to plenty of backlash and cynicism, though, and would have been less effective. As I explain in a later chapter, it sometimes is acceptable to promote a point of view, but Dorschner was wise to remain basically objective in this story.

There's a last positive point I want to make about this story. You may think "Stayin' Alive" reads a bit like a profile, especially of Marilyn Van Houten. Because we're always going to include the 5 W's and H (the inverted pyramid) in any story, it's fair enough to say this story tells us "who" it is about.

But there's really more going on here than that. Marilyn Van Houten is the driver; her actions, as much as the deterioration in her husband's condition and the games health care providers play, move this story along. You can make sense of a complex story, and stay on track, if you follow the driver.

Now, having heaped such lavish praise on this story, let me acknowledge what some might perceive as a major sleight of hand in its structure. It is only near the very end of the story that we are told Marilyn has been seeking home health care all along, and then it is only in the Epilogue that we learn she got it!

I know plenty of city editors who would have insisted that Dorschner tell the readers up front, at or near the very top of his story, that Ed Van Houten's long struggle for home health care was recently rewarded when the Metro-Dade county government decided to step in and foot the bill for him. These city editors would have insisted, in other words, that Dorschner start the story with the conclusion first!

They'd have a point, too. After all, when you read a game story dealing with your favorite team, you don't expect the reporter to give you a blow-by-blow account, but save the final score until the ending. You'd expect to know the score up front—inverted pyramid style—followed by details. Yet true storytelling technique always saves the best for last, and Dorschner seems justified in withholding the climax of his story until the ending. You be the judge.

ASSIGNMENT

I want you to select the most complex issue facing you (your friends, your community, or the nation) that you feel you could effectively report on. (You may think nuclear proliferation is the major issue, but you may be ill equipped to tackle such a story, so don't.)

Let's say, for the sake of an example, that you think teen pregnancy is a huge issue that's little understood by the public-at-large. In fact, it is an important issue: In some inner-city neighborhoods most of the births are to unmarried teens. We no longer use the term "illegitimate births," but they're almost always problem births anyway.

You won't have any trouble finding statistics for this story, from U.S. Census data to local county health records to any good yearbook or almanac.

You won't have any trouble identifying expert sources to interview, either, from high school guidance counselors to volunteers at teen clubs and shelters to social workers at area hospitals to county health department officials.

You won't have problems locating background reading material: Just do a keyword search in any appropriate online database with the following keywords: teen pregnancy.

And you shouldn't have much trouble locating a teen mother or two to focus on. Many school districts have "alternative" schools that cater in part to teen moms; you might be allowed in to speak to one. Your local welfare department might be willing to let you interview a teen mother, too. Or, just hang out at any apartment complex in your town. Many of the units will be rented to single mothers, and some of those will be teen moms.

Talk to several teen moms (or pregnant teens about to give birth) until you find one or two with whom you're really comfortable, and who are comfortable with you. You want someone with decent communication and verbal skills who can sustain a long "focus" structure piece. Try to identify the father, too, if at all possible, and talk at length to him as well. Be prepared to spend time with your primary sources. If you're doing this assignment as part of a college course, start your research early in the semester! Do you think John Dorschner just sat down with Marilyn and Ed for a couple of hours and came away with a great story?

When it comes time to write your story, especially as it's likely to be a complicated one, you may want to start out simply, like Dorschner did, and summarize the main issues in the story before going off into the details of your primary source's life. But overall, you will tell me of the trials and tribulations of being a young single mom or pregnant teen, and you will feed me the statistics and expert quotes only as they are required during the narrative. Do not, I repeat, do not, submit a "term paper" on teen pregnancy that's merely sandwiched between a little profile of some young woman. The kind of sandwich structure we noted in shorter trend stories will not work well with a true focus structure. You have to focus on your main subject or subjects throughout the course of the story. In other words, do what Dorschner does.

6

Problems and Solutions

I first began emphasizing this technique in the fall of 1988, after one of the greatest droughts of the 20th century. Dozens of states suffered through scores of days with temperatures in the high 90s and above, and farmers across the country went weeks without significant rainfall to drench their crops. Almost all the grass along Indiana's extensive state highway system died; the corn crop looked more like yellow-brown confetti than a real grain by August and September of that year. Many farmers left the land; small businesses that catered to farmers were also hurt, and food prices at the grocery stores jumped.

The "problem" in the above scenario, of course, was the devastation caused by the drought (and, perhaps, lack of preparedness for it, such as lack of modern irrigation equipment).

The "solution" would be what the farmers did as a consequence of the drought, as well as what the local bankers and county agricultural extension office and government bureaucrats did about it. In 1988, some farmers just up and quit, of course; maybe they sold out to large farm conglomerates, who operate with increased numbers of low-cost migrant laborers or further mechanize the farming industry. Some small banks went out of business when creditors defaulted on loans, or they started making more nonagricultural loans.

Maybe some farmers started a local support group, which would be interesting because farmers aren't known as "touchy-feely" types; perhaps some farm wives went to work in town to help support their families. (Actually, many farm wives and husbands already had additional jobs in the city, but the drought may have accelerated the trend, thereby further degrading the quality and tradition of rural agricultural life.)

78

Maybe the government kicked in with low-cost loans to help out. But that implies an increase in the national debt, which some politicians have been fighting to cap and reduce in recent years. There are as many problems as there are solutions.

Before this starts to sound too much like an agribusiness story, let me remind you that there are some real dynamics here that touch real people's lives. As long as you don't forget that, you'll have a fine human interest feature story. You might, for example, begin such a story on the drought of 1988 (or 2008—there's sure to be more) by focusing on one farm family—how they've been hit by the crisis and what they're going to do about it. Then you would expand your story to look at other farmers and businesses and agencies affected, and what they are doing about it.

William Blundell (1988, pp. 74–75) emphasizes a similar journalistic model in his excellent *The Art and Craft of Feature Writing*. He refers to "impacts" and "countermoves."

Think of the 1988 drought as "news."

Then ask yourself, "Who was impacted by the news? And, what were their countermoves—what did they do about their problems? And why weren't people prepared for this development in the first place? Also, are the solutions working? If not, why not?" Follow this train of thought and answer questions like these, and you've got a story.

Here's another example. The largest television manufacturing plant in the United States, located in Bloomington, Indiana, is about to close. True story: RCA, which is now a French-owned company, is moving the plant to Mexico. The big news here is the global economy and the impact of NAFTA, the North American Free Trade Agreement, but the local story is that one of the city's very largest employers is leaving town.

The problem: Factory is closing, throwing hundreds out of work.

The solution: Well, we don't know what the solution is yet, but that's what local reporters are exploring in their continuing coverage of the imminent event.

This is all pretty straightforward, I feel, but let's complicate things just a bit.

Problems: More than 1,200 people will lose their jobs when the RCA factory closes; county tax coffers will lose millions of dollars annually; property values on the southwest part of town, where many of the workers and managers live, will take a big hit; the United Way charitable organization will lose hundreds of thousands of dollars in contributions annually, affecting agencies like the battered women's shelter and the Salvation Army.

Solutions: Not so easy to detect, frankly. People who lose their jobs may lose their homes if they can't pay the mortgage, but enlightened bankers typically will refinance mortgages to make payments easier. This is one solution you might write about.

And another factory might want to move into the old TV manufacturing building. I know when a national tire manufacturer moved out of Bloomington a decade ago, a smaller, regional tire company set up shop in the old factory. Not as many people were employed, and the pay wasn't as good, but it was something. Partial solution.

Another solution comes in the form of job fairs and retraining programs for the former RCA employees, perhaps funded by the state department of labor and/or federal agencies. In fact, this was part of the solution in Bloomington, and *The* (Bloomington) *Herald-Times* gave good coverage to these retraining efforts. (Obviously, this was part of continuing coverage of a major story, not part of a single story on a single event.)

Some workers, of course, will move. Some managers probably are studying Spanish right now and will move to Mexico with the factory. That's a solution for select individuals you would include in the story.

Even the United Way Agency had a partial solution: RCA executives recently agreed to a "settlement" that will give United Way some money even after RCA is gone, but only for a while.

Of course, solutions don't always work out. Welfare reform currently is a hot topic in America and will continue to be so for several years. Most states have been given 5 years, as of 1996 and 1997, to move a specified number of welfare clients off the welfare rolls and into jobs.

The problem: Too many people on welfare, not enough money to keep paying them.

The solution: Welfare reform.

But ...

This is a good story to follow up on because welfare reform has been tried in the past, with mixed results, and it's not possible that all the proposed reforms and solutions will work this time, either.

So, you can focus on one single mom or one agency that works with welfare moms and see what they're doing to accommodate the push for welfare reform. Maybe you'll visit an adult basic education class or a resume-writing class, just to see how things are going and how people are feeling.

But you may get statistics that show a kind of recidivism for welfare clients: They may get off welfare for a while, but fall back on it in a few months. This is where you go from problem to solution to problem again (because the company that employed the ex-welfare clients went out of business, or because state and federal aid dried up for the makeshift program into which the welfare client was thrust).

You may find that local welfare reform efforts are failing, but get a tip that there are really good programs in a neighboring community or state. Will your editor let you go on an overnighter to investigate the other solutions? He or she should.

In doing a story like this, you might focus on one mother. You can tell her story of dropping out of school and having children out of wedlock, but you will also include the hardship of finding child care and transportation so she can get to her adult basic education or resume-writing class.

Then you can include the statistics on the number of people taken off the welfare rolls, the new jobs created, or the recidivism rate. Beware, though, because people are going to ply you with misleading statistics. Still, a sparse use of valid statistics can give you the big picture in a hurry, very much like in the John Dorschner story in the previous chapter.

In outlining your story, you may start with an anecdotal lead focusing on one person or entity, but after that you almost always will follow with (a) the problems your subjects face, (b) the proposed and attempted solutions, and (c) the problems with those solutions, if any.

Here's a story from *The Wall Street Journal.* It's bit trend story, bit business story. But, for our purposes in this chapter, it's about a wine marketing problem—getting young Americans to drink more wine—and attempted solutions.

~~∾~~

Swallowing Hard
Wine Gets a Makeover: A Complex Zinfandel Becomes a Power 'Zin'
With Consumption Flat, Vintners Plan Flashy Ads To Lure Leery Gen-Xers
'Take It Off Its Pedestal'*
by Elizabeth Jensen

At the Best Cellars wine store on New York's Upper East Side, there isn't a bottle of expensive Chateau Margaux to be found. Instead, shoppers find 100 good, mostly lesser-known wines, not one with a price-tag over $10.

Joshua Wesson and Richard Marmet, who opened the store last fall and hope it will be the prototype for a national chain, are betting that Americans are ripe for a pared-down approach to buying wine. Displayed in spare, backlit columns in a setting that looks remarkably like a Gap store, Best Cellars' carefully edited inventory is grouped not by country of origin, but by color and taste, such as "juicy" or "fizzy." The idea is to make wine-buying fun, simple and "bomb-proof," says Mr. Wesson, a longtime sommelier and wine consultant who saw an untapped market in consumers who find wine off-putting.

The $12.4 billion wine industry has had exactly the same epiphany.

"It's time for us to take wine off its pedestal and place it squarely on weekday family dinner tables, right alongside the microwaved macaroni and cheese," said R. Michael Mondavi, president and chief executive of Robert Mondavi Corp., in a speech to the Wine and Spirits Wholesalers of America in May.

---

*From "Swallowing Hard Wine Gets a Makeover: A Complex Zinfandel becomes a Power 'Zin' With Consumption Flat, Vintners Plan Flashy Ads To Lure Leery Gen-Xers 'Take It Off Its Pedestal' " by E. Jensen. *The Wall Street Journal,* Copyright © 1997, Dow Jones & Compny, Inc. All rights reserved worldwid.

Flurry of Initiatives

Faced with an increasingly narrow customer base and the specter of a glut in grapes, winemakers have launched a flurry of initiatives aimed at reversing their product's snob image as a complicated beverage with strict rules for enjoyment. Their goal: to persuade Americans that wine is a casual, everyday libation to be drunk like bottle water, beer or soda.

Consumers are thus being blitzed with everything from a Gen-X wine magazine to "Wine 101," a series for public television demystifying wine, to a campaign encouraging people to think of wine as celebrities: sauvingnon blanc as, say, lean peppy Jamie Lee Curtis or chardonnay as voluptuous, blond Marilyn Monroe.

In their biggest undertaking, the industry is laying plans to spend as much as $20 million a year for its first national generic TV-ad campaign, enlisting Bozell Worldwide, the New York ad agency that created the Milk Mustache and "Pork: The Other White Meat," to come up with a whimsical concept to give wine a feel-good image for a mass audience.

This is all in response to a few obvious realities. Although wine is enjoying a modest resurgence after a decade-long slip from a 1982 peak in consumption, a cruel fact looms: The vast majority of wine is drunk by a small group of dedicated Boomers—and they aren't getting any younger. The rest of the population—particularly 20- and 30-year-olds who are tomorrow's market—are often intimidated by all the complex talk of varietals, appellations and vintages.

Chris Begley, 31, shopping for wine on a Friday night at Best Cellars, typifies the problem. Unlike with vodka, "with wine, you never know what you're getting," she says. "You don't want to spend $10 or more on something if you don't know whether you'll like it. Buying wine takes a certain amount of knowledge."

"Good Cocktail Party Word"

Indeed, young investment bankers and lawyers with a lot of disposable income flood classes held by Kevin Zraly, wine director at Windows on the World in New York's World Trade Center. "They're taking my course because they're insecure," about wine, he says. "If they're feeling insecure, then can you imagine what the average person thinks?"

In a recent class, the fast-talking Mr. Zraly explained phylloxera, a microscopic pest that kills vines and led to a recent grape shortage, calling it "a good cocktail party word." He noted that the only problem with German wines is "unpronounceable names." One student, Daniel Sarana, 33, took the class because he is "always embarrassed about not knowing what wine to ask for." Jennifer Baldinger, 27, enrolled with her husband, Howard, after "an unbelievable amount of frustration" ordering wines while on their honeymoon in Italy. Though she calls herself "a beer drinker at heart," Ms. Baldinger says she and her husband go to fancy restaurants frequently, "and you can't exactly go to Le Cirque and order a beer."

Luring Younger Drinkers

A study earlier this year by the industry-funded Wine Market Council showed that a mere 11 percent of the nation's 21-to-59-year-olds drinks 88 percent of the table wine consumed. And while per-capita consumption has crept up steadily since 1991 to 2.26 gallons per person, it is still far below the 1982 high of 2.58 gallons, according to Adams Media figures. Moreover, almost all of the increased consumption is coming from people who are already core wine drinkers—those who drink wine at least once a week, says John Gillespie, president of the council, which is sponsoring the Bozell campaign.

The solution as many see it is to lure marginal consumers, as well as younger drinkers like Ms. Begley or Ms. Baldinger. But winemakers are starting their ad blitz just as regulators are closely scrutinizing alcohol marketing. Other factors work against them: For many families, sitting down for even macaroni and cheese dinners is a rare occasion. Wine packaging discourages consumers who want to have just a glass or two, and retailers are reluctant to carry half-bottles.

In addition, winemakers tread a thin line between trying to expand the market and cheapening their product's image with ad gimmicks. Big wineries are generally united in their support of a makeover; others aren't so sure. For "everyday wines, the less frightening approach is very important," and novice drinkers may eventually appreciate finer wines, says Sandra Maclver, president of Matanzas Creek Winery in Santa Rosa, Calif. "But when you get up into our wines, which run from $18 to $125 a bottle, I worry about taking away too much of the mystery and allure. There's a lot that goes into making our wines; they're complex and we want people to pay attention to the unique elements."

Grape Glut

Lending even more urgency to vintners' sense that they need to shift gears is the projected glut in U.S. grape production by the turn of the century. The prediction is based on a few factors. For one, vines planted to replace phylloxera-infested roots are expected to soon start producing large quantities. The acreage devoted to grapes has also expanded significantly, as more farmers join the wine business. And growers are using new techniques to double grape yields.

To keep prices from tumbling, analysts figure the industry needs to raise per capita wine consumption by as much as 15 percent annually for the next few years. "If we think we can sit here and expect prices to

remain stable in light of increased production, we're sadly mistaken,"
says Barry Bedwell, president of Allied Grape Growers, a Fresno, Calif., marketing cooperative. "We have to grow consumption."

Even before the generic campaign kicks in, wineries are stepping
up advertising. This year, Brown-Forman Corp.'s Fetzer Vineyards
launched its first-ever TV-ad campaign, spending $7 million, a huge
sum by industry standards; by comparison, leading producer E. & J.
Gallo Winery, one of the few vintners to regularly advertise on television, spent $12.3 million on TV ads last year, according to Competitive
Media Reporting, followed by Sebastiani Vineyards, at $3.1 million.

"Forget the Rules!"

Most of the new ads tout wine with a more accessible, fun image, such
as Sebastiani's $5 million campaign for its Nathanson Creek brand
("Plan to be Spontaneous"). The print campaign for Gallo's Ecco
Domani brand shows a young woman kicking up her heels, with the
copy "Red wine is for meat. White wine is for fish. Blah! blah! blah!
blah! Forget the rules! Enjoy the wine."

New print and TV ads for Gallo's Sonoma Estate Wines feature the
Gallo families' 30-something third-generation of winemakers. "We're
very conscious of the aging of the wine consumer and the need to at-
tract younger adults," says Patrick Dodd, director of marketing, of the
decision to use "our own generation of Gen-Xers who are entering into
major executive positions at the company."

Advertising, however, may have actually contributed to some of the
wine's current dilemma. The most memorable U.S. wine campaign
ever was Orson Welles intoning, "We will sell no wine before its time,"
for the Paul Masson brand in the late seventies, and the image stuck;
of wine as a special-occasion drink, which should be drunk in the right
year, using appropriate glasses, paired with the right food.

Mr. Mondavi traces the intimidation problem even further back, to
post-Prohibition. With Americans shut out of the business for so long,
he says, the British moved in, with formal rules about where and how
wine should be stored and drunk, and an obsession with expensive
French Bordeaux wines, many of which need years of aging before being ready to drink. "The American consumer, when given all these rules,
said, 'To hell with it; give me a beer, a scotch, a cup of coffee,'" he says.

Then, "there's that whole ritual in restaurants," says Jon
Fredrikson, of Gomber, Fredrikson & Associates, San Francisco
wine-industry economists. "With what else," he asks, "is there a person standing over you, say, checking if your steak is OK before you
spit it out?"

Guerilla Tactics

After a burst of advertising in the late 1970s and early 1980s helped
persuade baby boomers to ask for a glass of chablis, pushing con-

sumption to its 1982 record, the industry stopped touting itself, except in specialized wine publications. An attempt to do an industrywide promotion for California wines in the late-1980s never got past the test stage because of internal bickering, and the campaign—one ad showed a man with his dog saying, "He drinks beer, I drink wine"—was viewed by many as a creative flop.

In one of the more unorthodox new efforts, a group of young winery employees started the nonprofit, industry-funded Wine Brats, an educational organization in Sonoma, Calif., in 1992; they have now added chapters in 32 cities. The group has been trying to woo young adults away from upscale tequilas and beer through tastings and on-line chats. One of the Wine Brat's first guerrilla attention-getters involved ambushing young diners in San Francisco's trendy Eleven restaurant to grill them about why they hadn't ordered a bottle of wine—and then challenge them to compare the taste of their meal with a glass of specially chosen wine vs. a soft-drink or beer.

And a who's who of industry sponsors, including the Wine Institute and the Napa and Sonoma valley vintners associations, helped fund the "Wine 101" public TV series. Narrated by David Hyde Pierce, the actor who plays Niles on the hit sitcom "Frasier," the series introduces basic wine terms and discusses how to enjoy, buy and store wine. "Don't let some techno-bourgeois-elitist-yuppie bore tell you how to taste wine!" is one of the show's rallying cries.

Sex, Wine & Rock 'n' Roll

Wine X, a new independently funded magazine for Generation X Wine drinkers, aims to make wine seem hip and accessible to younger consumers. Daryl M. Roberts, editor and publisher, says it isn't for connoisseurs who want obscure bottlings like "the second harvest night picking, second vine from the left behind the barn." With the requisite chaotic jumble of typefaces, Wine-X launched its first color issue this summer, proclaiming in the publisher's letter: "The era of elitist and pretentious wine publications is over." The first issue features snowboarders talking about wine. Another article, "Sex, Wine & Rock 'n' Roll," suggests "a complex cab or a powerful zin from Clos du Val" as the beverage to drink when listening to the "easily digestible beats simmered against dance-floor friendly grooves" on the new album from the electronic-pop group Orb.

But the timing of all the efforts aimed at increasing consumption, particularly among young people, is less than ideal, in the wake of the crackdown on the tobacco industry's marketing practices to hook young smokers. Unlike beer, wine—a beverage that largely appeals to a small group of well-off adults—has always been above the fray. By attempting to boost demand and make itself more of a mass-market product, wineries are now putting themselves smack in the middle of the debate over whether promoting alcoholic drinks stimulates alcohol abuse.

The industry already is drawing intense scrutiny for its proposal to put labels on bottles referring to the health effects of wine, a plan that has drawn fierce opposition from public-health organizations. The label, developed by the Wine Institute, the California vintners' lobbying organization, would direct consumers to write for the 1995 U.S. Dietary Guidelines "to learn the health effects of moderate wine consumption." Those guidelines say that moderate consumption of alcohol, defined as a drink a day for women and two drinks for men, can be part of a healthy diet.

The Wine Institute lobbied heavily to get those benefits included in the guidelines, and aggressively publicized positive scientific studies, particularly the "French Paradox" report of 1991, which linked lower rates of heart disease in France with red-wine consumption. These reports were largely responsible for the turnaround in the decade-long decline in per capita consumption. Baby boomers "drink wine without guilt," Mr. Fredrikson says, where "10 years ago, wine was basically a recreational drug."

Wine marketers say they are fully aware of public-health sensitivities in trying to increase consumption. The approach being considered by the Wine Market Council encourages moderation, "wine consumed by adults in adult situations," Mr. Gillespie says. "You won't see a Swedish bikini team (in these ads).... If you act responsibly and credibly you have nothing to fear."

～.～～

Initiatives, efforts, approaches, solutions: These are all words that actually appear in the above text that explicitly tell you this is a problems and solutions story.

Note the theme statement (also known as a nut graf), which comes right after the anecdotal lead and the first subhead:

> Faced with an increasingly narrow customer base and the specter of a glut in grapes, winemakers have launched a flurry of initiatives aimed at reversing their product's snob image as a complicated beverage with strict rules for enjoyment. Their goal: to persuade Americans that wine is a casual, everyday libation to be drunk like bottled water, beer or soda.

There's the problem in a nutshell, with the writer's promise to discuss several "initiatives" (read: solutions) in the remainder of the story.

Note a few paragraphs down in the story from the nut graf, where the author writes about "a few obvious realities." These include information that wine consumption peaked in 1982 and the claim that 20-somethings and 30-somethings are not drinking much wine at all; it's just the aging

Baby Boomers who keep sales up. More problems, obviously, or rather proof that a problem exists.

Yet other problems are documented in this story. "There's that whole ritual in restaurants" that many people find off-putting, the author quotes one source as saying. Then there's the fear of being compared to the tobacco industry.

The "solutions" are all over this story, too, from *Wine 101*, the public television show, to Wine Brats, an organization with chapters in 32 cities and growing. There are several other proposed solutions in the story as well.

Yet, as noted in the introduction to this chapter, some solutions come with their own problems, and the author does not ignore this in discussing wine sales. For example, find the line that reads, "But winemakers are starting their ad blitz just as regulators are closely scrutinizing alcohol marketing" for allegedly encouraging alcohol abuse. The same paragraph also notes that any ad campaign targeting dinnertime as wine time is in trouble, because many families don't sit down to dinner together anyway. Put another way, the author is saying that increased advertising is no magic bullet for the wine industry.

A few paragraphs down, the author notes that past advertising was so successful in creating snob appeal ("We will sell no wine before it's time") that making wine a cool, casual drink will prove to be a tall order (pun intended; sorry).

Anyway, I think you get the picture.

Let me add one more note about this story. The use of quotes is quite good. Although I generally don't like partial quotes (also known as quote fragments), that is, quoting a part of someone's statement inside your own sentence, the author does this well here, limiting her quotes to what is really quite colorful language, such as the quote about "dance-floor friendly grooves" and including the slogan, "Don't let some techno-bourgeois-elitist-yuppie bore tell you how to taste wine!" (Right on! If Mountain Dew made a chardonnay, these people would drink it.)

I think the best quote, because it was colorful and impossible to paraphrase, was this: "With what else," (asks Jon Frederikson, of Gomber, Frederikson, & Associates, San Francisco wine-industry economists), "is there a person standing over you, say, checking if your steak is OK before you spit it out?"

Now, there is another kind of "problems and solutions" approach I want to introduce here. This has emerged in recent years in the debate over what is known as "public journalism" or "civic journalism." In a nutshell, public or civic journalism seeks to focus attention on the major issues of the day (crime, health care reform, racism and inequality, declining educational standards, rebuilding inner cities, the loss of good-paying factory jobs to foreign competition), or on important local issues (water resources in the Southwest, unsafe nuclear power stations in Illinois, school consolidation anywhere), with a view toward presenting competing solutions, or at least improving the quality of debate on the issues. One sometimes sees a public journalism or civic journalism approach in coverage of major elections: The candidates may have their own talking points, but a lot of journalists and editors feel it is their right (obligation, even) to identify the real issues and press candidates to take meaningful stands on them.

In a sense, the new emphasis on public and civic journalism looks a little like the old "advocacy journalism," which will be discussed at length in the chapter on Point of View. Such a comparison is debatable, though. Proponents of public and civic journalism deny they are forcing any point of view or any specific set of solutions on anyone; instead they boast that they are demanding that responsible leaders address the big issues and propose their own solutions, which can then be scrutinized.

Some people write about public journalism with great fervor. "Public journalism is ... a confrontation with a long-suppressed fact: The press is a participant in our national life" (cited in Balough, 1996, p. 21). So wrote Jay Rosen, associate professor of journalism at New York University in 1996.

Not everyone agrees with this emphasis on public journalism, of course: "News reporters are supposed to explore the issues, not solve them. Newspapers are supposed to expose the wrongs, not campaign against them" (cited in Bbalough, 1996, p. 22). So wrote Michael Gartner, chairman and editor of *The Daily Tribune* in Ames, Iowa, in rebuttal to Rosen.

ASSIGNMENT

Well, here's your assignment: Write a problem-solution story. Your outline can be as simple as this:

1. Anecdotal lead.
2. Nut graf, which introduces problem and possible solutions.
3. More specifics on problems.
4. Proposed solutions.
5. Unintended consequences; some problems with those solutions.
6. Ending.

If this is too abstract, think of the problem of, say, gambling on college campuses. The anecdotal lead can look at a young male student (almost always a male, frankly), who's frittering away his money and time on cards, the ponies, or point spreads on basketball games when he should be studying. Maybe the scene is of the young man having an emotional breakdown back in his dorm room after he realizes how much money he's lost.

The nut graf will summarize the problem, perhaps with an estimate of the number of student gamblers and a statement to the effect that university administrators are aware and increasingly concerned with this problem.

The body of the story can look more closely at all the ways students gamble, or at other students' stories of gambling excesses. You might quote an expert or two to the effect that this is really, really a problem.

Then, you look at specific efforts individual students, as well as the universities on an institutional level, are taking to curb gambling. Is confidential counseling offered to such students? Are there public information campaigns against gambling on campus? Maybe visit a Gamblers Anonymous group and include that briefly in your story.

But not all these efforts will be effective, so you might as well admit to the failed solutions, too. Perhaps the state is licensing more gambling casinos even as it claims to be concerned about gamblers of all ages.

The ending can go right back to the person you introduced in the lead, or you might have an ominous quote from someone saying the problem is only going to get worse unless more is done to combat it.

7

The Journalistic Essay

Some thinkers divide all newspaper articles into two types: Deadline and nondeadline.

Deadline stories—auto crashes, crime scene reports, stock market rallies, the sudden death of a famous person—are the bread-and-butter of journalism. The inverted pyramid is tailor-made for handling difficult copy under the press of deadline. *Who was killed at the intersection of Main and Spring streets yesterday? What time did the accident occur? How, and why? Were the streets slick with ice?*

Everything else is nondeadline. That includes not only personality profiles and trend stories in the feature section, but TV, movie, and art reviews, as well as editorials and political columns on the op-ed pages.

If you can accept this severe dichotomy, then the essay as a journalistic tool will not be so difficult to swallow. It's part editorial, part personal column, part review of literature, part original investigation, part news summary, and part lots of other things. Perhaps it differs from a feature story most in that features have a story to tell; essays have a point to make.

In any case, the first step in understanding the journalistic essay is to note that it is not a deadline story, hence it is part of that universe into which we toss all nondeadline stories.

One of my favorite contemporary news essayists is John Leo, who writes for *U.S. News & World Report* and syndicates a national column. His essays are considered political, but not in the sense of supporting this or that candidate or movement. He's always struck me as a "classical liberal," that is, a person who supports the rights of the individual, free speech, and spirited debate, and smaller government. (If you think "smaller government" and "liberal" are contradictory terms, just read some of Thomas Jefferson's writings, or earlier writings by the English philosopher John Locke, who sought to limit the power and influence of royal government.)

I've seen John Leo also referred to as a "neo-conservative." He often writes about what he perceives as political correctness on campus and alleged excesses of what he has labeled race, gender, and victim ideology.

I like John Leo because he's the little child who cried, "The emperor's not wearing any new clothes," except that the little child is all grown up now.

He's billed as a columnist, and like a good columnist he has the ability to speak directly to you, the reader. But he writes the essay. He cites documents and quotes from them in his essays, and he quotes individuals with relevant things to say. This is what any good reporter should do. Leo observes, and quotes, and cites, and jabs. He challenges both conventional wisdom and the reader to think for himself or herself. But he—John Leo—doesn't try to remain invisible in the essay. You know it's a John Leo essay when you're finished, and you know what John Leo thinks.

The following essay was written in the aftermath of a controversy over a proposed exhibit at the Smithsonian Institution in Washington to commemorate the end of World War II in the Pacific and the dropping of the atomic bomb on Hiroshima in 1945. The Enola Gay was the name given to the heavy bomber that carried the payload over Hiroshima. Some observers felt the exhibit as originally planned blamed the United States for unnecessarily dropping the bomb, and for doing so only because the Japanese were of a different race. The critics said the exhibit was entirely one-sided and anti-American. Defenders of the exhibit said they were trying to present a different point of view than the one allegedly usually seen in U.S. history books.

~~~~~

Enola, we hardly knew ye*
by John Leo

With each new essay and book on the Enola Gay controversy, the conventional story line about the canceled exhibit seems a bit shakier. That story line, set in concrete in the academic world and most of the media, says that a straightforward Smithsonian show about the plane that dropped the atomic bomb on Hiroshima was defeated by a backward-looking alliance of veterans and superpatriots.

But there's doubt about how straightforward the exhibit was meant to be. "History Wars," a collection of essays mostly about the Enola Gay exhibit, contains a reference to "trial balloons" sent up my Martin Harwit, then director of the Smithsonian's Air and Space Museum. Edward Linenthal, a historian friendly to Harwit, wrote that the director saw some

---

*From "Enola, we hardly knew ye" by J. Leo. Copyright © Dec. 1, 1997, U.S. News & World Report. Reprinted by permission.

of the museum's provocative new exhibits as "trial balloons" intended to change Air and Space "from a temple to a forum." The word "temple" is a common disparaging term used by historians and curators who dislike the unadorned display of famous aircraft and spacecraft at the museum. It invites, they say, simple admiration instead of critical thinking about the negative effects of aerospace technology.

This "anti-temple" thinking colored the approach to the Enola Gay exhibit. In his book, "An Exhibit Denied," Harwit says many people at the museum feared that "a massive, gleaming Enola Gay would give the impression that the museum was celebrating raw power." Unable to ponder the plane correctly, the masses would need expert help from the museum in understanding what it all meant.

Harwit told me he doesn't recall using the words "trial balloons," but he considers it a good term for what was happening. One trial balloon was an exhibit of Nazi V-2 rockets that showed photos of dead bodies (the first ever at the museum) and explained at length (and somewhat irrelevantly) that forced labor had been used to manufacture the missiles. The show also made an obvious editorial point about Wernher von Braun, showing side-by-side photos of him helping the Nazis during the war and the Americans afterward.

Bigger balloons. With its hectoring moral tone and its determination to tell us how to feel, the V-2 show might have raised some eyebrows but didn't, possibly because the pro-Nazi lobby in Washington is small. "Nobody objected," Harwit says with relief in his book. And few objected after the more serious balloons that Harwit's team sent up. The museum's space shows "Exploring New Worlds" and "Where Next, Columbus?" condemned Europe's "invasion" and "frantic exploration and exploitation" of the Americas and suggested that the same horrid things might be taking place in space. One display raised the deep question, "Does Mars Have Rights?" and asked, "Is human exploration of Mars an act of destiny or arrogance?" (Hint: For the correct answer, try "arrogance.")

An exhibit of World War I aircraft also demonstrated that curators were unable to keep their political opinions out of shows. John Correll, editor of Air Force magazine, correctly called the show a "strident attack on air power in World War I." Determined to erase what one curator called "the spirit of romance" that surrounds pilots of that war, the show went weirdly out of its way to disparage Germany's ace, the Red Baron.

The Enola Gay show, at one point envisioned as an exhibit to be called "From Guernica to Hiroshima—Bombing in World War II," was a follow-up to the World War I show. The "dark shadow" cast by the rise of air power in the first show would become, in Linenthal's words, "a shadow growing every larger and darker" in the second. This helps explain a lot of the friction surrounding the Enola Gay show. The museum not only decided to use Hiroshima to mark the 50th celebration of the Allied victory, itself a very aggressive and revealing decision. But it also planned to mount the show against a background of sharply hostile staff opinions about air power and Harwit's own strong antinuclear stance.

Harwit says his policy was not to tell visitors what to think. But the ideological smog was so thick at Air and Space that disaster was bound to occur. As a Washington Post editorial said, the museum showed a "curatorial inability to perceive that political opinions are embedded in the exhibit, or to identify them as such—opinions—rather than universal objective assumptions that all thinking people must necessarily share." Similar criticism comes in a new book by a Smithsonian anthropologist. In "Reflections of a Culture Broker," Richard Kurin says the curators "naively believed that there is an absolute historical truth" and dismissed opponents as being motivated by politics rather than a legitimate difference of opinion.

The point is not that the curators were wrong about the Enola Gay. The obliteration of a nonstrategic city filled mostly with women and children raises some obvious moral problems. But the state and its employees are not supposed to tell us how to think or feel about it. Nothing irritates the citizens more than being propagandized with their own tax money. Given the ideological currents flowing through the museum, this issue will surely come up again and again until the curators get it right.

Note that this is not merely an editorial. It is historically characteristic of editorials to either support or disapprove of various policies, actions, candidates, exhibits, or whatever. It is also not a personal column; John Leo is not merely sharing his feelings on the matter. Rather, he is taking you on a tour of the issues behind the issues. It's clear to me he would have supported an evenhanded, balanced presentation on the dropping of the Atomic Bomb that may indeed have ruffled some feathers. I certainly would have supported such a presentation. But it's also clear that Leo thinks the exhibit was never going to be evenhanded or balanced, and he has convinced me of that by his excellent and incisive reporting and writing.

Here's another journalistic essay, also about a controversial topic. How do you write about slavery more than 125 years after it's been outlawed in the United States? Who will be in your lead? Who will you interview? A traditional feature story approach may not work. But it's an eminently valid topic, one of burning interest to millions of Americans still. Of course any editorial on the subject is going to condemn slavery. Perhaps some articles will resurrect the tales of people, long deceased now, who lived through slavery. One way to give voice to a story on slavery would be to excerpt old diaries and letters written by slaves themselves: I have seen this technique used to good effect, both in print and in filmed documentaries.

The essay is another good tool to employ in tackling such an important and sensitive topic. You can draw from any source or resource you need; you are not bound, as it were, by the need for an overly dramatic or "feature-y" lead. The pressure is off for literary-type writing style; clarity and focus will do.

Here's the essay on slavery, or rather a current topic related to its long, sad history, from a printed source that might surprise you, but shouldn't.

~·~·~

Slavery: Nations Built on Brutality; Slavery took a huge social and economic toll on its victims. Now some people want this historic debt repaid.*
by Joseph Harker

Estimates vary, but somewhere between 20 and 100 million people were either enslaved or killed in Africa and the Americas during the slave trade. But in addition to this human tragedy, the trade also had a huge economic impact in the three continents involved.

In the Americas, slavery brought huge wealth to plantation owners. But slaves never benefitted from the profits of their labour. After arriving in the Americas, they were made to reject their links with Africa. They were brutally treated to break their spirits and then forced to adapt to new working and living conditions, to learn a new language and adopt new customs. This process, known as "seasoning," often lasted two or three years. Already weakened by the trauma of their voyage, many died or committed suicide; others resisted and were punished.

To justify this treatment, Africans were portrayed by slaveholders as an inferior race. Even after the abolition of slavery, the southern black population was segregated and given a low standard of education for a further 100 years. And the lasting effects of this lived on in the poverty of many African Americans and the discrimination against them which still continues.

In European countries, the huge profits made from the sale of commodities from the Americas helped to boost the whole economy. The slave and sugar trade made Bristol Britain's second city for the first three-quarters of the 18th century.

Sugar and cotton formed the basis of large industries across England, and by 1750 there was hardly a trading or manufacturing town in England which was not in some way connected to the triangular trade. In London, insurance and banking companies depended on the trade. Lloyd's insured slaves and slave ships. Two members of the Barclays family were also involved in the slave trade.

---

*From "Slavery: Nations Built on Brutality; Slavery took a huge social and economic toll on its victims. Now some people want this historic debt repaid." by Joseph Harker. Copyright © 1994. *The Guardian* (London).

Eric Williams, the former prime minister of Trinidad, in his book "Capitalism and Slavery," said of the trade: "The profits obtained provided one of the main streams of that accumulation of capital in England which financed the industrial revolution." Meanwhile, in Africa, the trade took its toll. Before the arrival of European slave-traders, its kingdoms and city-states traded in gold, bronze and ivory goods. Art, learning and technology flourished. The impact of the slave trade on African political organisation and on its economy and society as a whole was immense.

Not only were millions of young people lost to the slave trade, but the firearms which were handed over by Europeans increased warfare and instability. During the 19th century, Europeans began to colonize Africa, and by the 1890s they had divided up almost the entire continent among themselves. They ran the newly formed countries to service their home economies, and benefitted from their resources.

Now the National Coalition of Blacks for Reparations in America (N'COBRA) is pushing for black Americans to receive compensation for slavery and the racial discrimination that followed. Prominent African-American leader Jesse Jackson believes a combination of housing, education and new jobs should be offered.

The movement began in earnest after 1988, when Japanese-Americans who had been imprisoned during the second world war received compensation. "Black people stayed in slavery for 246 years," says Raymond Jenkins, head of the Detroit branch of N'COBRA. "Japanese people were in camps for three years and got $20,000." In Britain, the reparations movement is backed by Labour MP Bernie Grant. One of its demands is for the cancellation of black Africa's trade debt. Already, 70 MPs have backed Grant's call, but the proposal has a long way to go before it might pass into law.

Nicholas Budgen, a Conservative MP, has said: "I don't think the British Government or the British people have got anything to apologise for at all. The idea of financial reparations is ludicrous." Others say that the technology which Europe brought to Africa left the continent in a better state than when they arrived. Whatever the case, there is no doubt that Europe can only look back on its involvement in slavery with a sense of shame.

Before we move on to the next example of a journalistic essay, some characteristics already should be clear: This essay has a point to make, and it's written with real force. The voice of authority comes through. In all this, it is somewhat like an editorial.

The essay also uses various facts and figures to bolster its case and can quote people; for example, the essayist sometimes turns reporter and interviews and quotes people directly in his or her text. Specifically, I like this essay from a famous English newspaper because it delves into a great human drama and tragedy unblinkingly and unsentimentally, but not un-emotionally. Eschewing a more "feature-y" approach, the author lets the facts and figures do the talking for him. It's not an approach that you, as a feature writer, will always use (remember the early admonition in this book to try and write the news from the vantage point of those affected by it), but sometimes the essay is a great technique when you just want to cut to the heart of the matter.

The third example of a journalistic essay deals with the environment.

~.~.~

Rethinking man's place: One Earth*
by Dianne Dumanoski

Those who take the environmental crisis seriously increasingly insist that the planet cannot take much more business as usual. Things have got to change.

But what things? What changes?

Is salvation to be found in technology, such as energy-efficient light bulbs and clean-burning liquid hydrogen to fuel our beloved cars? Or is it in new laws and long jail terms for polluters? Can we tax our way to a saner future by stiff levies on fossil fuels? Do we need a global treaty so we can be sure everyone will do the right thing?

Taxes and technology, legislation and treaties. These tend to be the boundaries of the mainstream debate about how to get our planet out of the mess it's in.

But outside this mainstream, a diverse chorus of voices is calling for another kind of change altogether. What we need most of all, they argue, is a revolution in our world view—a different view of nature and of our place in it. Only then, they say, can we find our way to a viable future.

Whatever they call themselves—deep ecologists, eco-feminists, neo-pagans, bioregionalists or believers in Earth First!—these voices condemn the prevailing "anthropocentric" view, which holds that humans are the measure of creation and regards the rest of the planet as resources for human use.

"The 'control of nature' is a phrase conceived in arrogance, born of the Neanderthal age of biology and philosophy, when it was supposed that nature exists for the convenience of man," wrote Rachel Carson in "Silent Spring" in 1962.

Carson, John Muir and Aldo Leopold are among the American environmental writers and thinkers in this century who have called for a humbler, ultimately wiser, view of ourselves and our place.

What we need, Leopold wrote in a classic essay, is to change "the role of Homo sapiens from conqueror of the land community of plants and animals to plain member and citizen of it. It implies a respect for

---

*From "Rethinking man's place: One Earth" by D. Dumanoski. Copyright © 1990, *The Boston Globe*. Reprinted by permission.

fellow members and also a respect for the community as such." At any rate, he wrote almost half a century ago, the conqueror approach has proved self-defeating. Contemporary environmental critics say this truth is only more undeniable today.

If humans are not, cannot be, the masters of creation, what should the relationship be? This is not just an environmental question. Many, including philosophers, spiritual leaders and mythology scholar Joseph Campbell, see this as the central cultural, spiritual and philosophical question of our time.

"We have today to learn to get back into accord with the wisdom of nature and realize again our brotherhood with the animals and with the water and the sea," said Campbell in his television series, the "Power of Myth."

"The only myth that is going to be worth thinking about in the immediate future is one that is talking about the planet ... and how to relate this society to the world of nature and the cosmos."

Campbell went on to read at length from a widely-quoted letter by the 19th century Suquamish Native American leader, Chief Seattle: "This we know: the Earth does not belong to the Man, man belongs to the Earth. All things are connected like the blood that unites us all. Man did not weave the web of life; he is merely a strand in it. Whatever he does to the web, he does to himself."

As it turns out, Seattle's letter, which has gained an almost scriptural significance among many striving to find a new relationship with nature, is largely a fabrication "recreated" by a Hollywood script writer in 1970. Whatever its origin, however, the letter has taken on a life of its own because it speaks so eloquently to deep concerns.

The search for a different relationship has taken many along a path they describe as "biocentric" or "ecocentric." In this view, plants and animals (and, for the ecocentrist, rivers and mountains) have equal value to humans and have an equal right to exist, live and flourish.

"To say that the human is not merely not the dominant species on Earth, but only one among all other species and equal to all other species—this is a hard idea for some people to live with," said author Kirkpatrick Sale, whose book "Dwellers in the Land: The Bioregional Vision," explores efforts to build a new relationship to nature. But hard as it may be, he argues, this new vision and the profound change in values that would accompany it are "the only solution. There is no other. Anthropocentric ways of thinking do not offer us a way out."

The implications of a biocentric vision are radical, since it would follow that humans have no right to reduce the diversity of nature, either directly or indirectly. Since this is impossible, deep ecologists acknowledge that limited use of nature is unavoidable.

"If you follow the logic of the argument out far enough, not being anthropocentric means not manipulating nature at all," observes Yale environmental historian William Cronon. "For the deep ecologist, the benign human relationship with nature is finally a hunter–gatherer."

Cronon says he is troubled by the emphasis on uninhabited wilderness by "deep ecology" thinkers, since it implies "the only nature worthy of our respect is where we are not living. If we live ethically, we ought to treat our backyard with the same respect as any wilderness area."

In his view, the idea of stewardship, which Leopold saw as the core of an environmental ethic, might be a more fruitful avenue in the search for a modus vivendi. Perhaps, he suggests, the idea of nurturing "in (the) way we nurture our garden or our children" might provide a sounder basis for this relationship.

Writer and farmer Wendell Berry may have pinpointed the inescapable bottom line in an essay called "Preserving Wildness." He wrote: "To use or not use nature is not a choice that is available to us; we can only live at the expense of other lives. Our choice has rather to do with how and how much to use."

Another history lesson, right? Essays often are like that. They're like a stern lecture, a good speech, even a jeremiad at times. The voice of "authority" that currently is bandied about in journalistic circles is heard in the above examples in part because their authors all appear to be well-read. They sound authoritative because they are authoritative. This is substance over style, not *vice versa*, which is another thing to like about journalistic essays.

The "One Earth" essay is particularly nice in that it may be partisan, but is in no way extreme. The author clearly supports environmental concerns, but doesn't believe in unrealistic expectations that we can all go back to the "hunter–gatherer" state. For example, she includes a great quote about those environmentalists who believe the only way nature should be is where humans don't exist!

There aren't the numbers in the "One Earth" essay that we find in the "Slavery" essay, for example, but there are plenty of quotes, aptly employed, that get the author's point across. The essay may seem on the surface to be like a long editorial, but it does employ traditional journalistic methods such as quoting experts.

Note that all the above essays differ from more typical journalistic features in that they don't include "real people" or ordinary person anecdotes. That's just the opposite of what you want to do most feature stories! Nevertheless, I find the essay to be quite liberating. You can go to the library and check out a whole host of sources; you can go to your favorite online database and search, search, search for just the information you need. Although it's true that everyone is entitled to his or her opinion, and that all opinions are valued, some opinions are more informed and learned than others. For better or worse, the essay typically swims in the waters of expert sources, not the common folk.

Some authors also find it liberating that you can adopt a point of view, take a stand, in many essays, although frequently essays are employed to give the "other side of the story" or to bring to the fore facts that may have been overlooked in deadline stories.

Special note: I've also seen this specific blending of journalistic and essayist techniques referred to as the *reported essay*, which can be like rather long, serious magazine articles. But this latter expression is not in common use, nor is there any consensus on just what the term "reported essay" means. At present, it is more of an academic term than one used by everyday journalists. Nevertheless, look at back issues of *The Atlantic Monthly* or *The New Yorker* for examples. You might look for articles by Joe Klein, who wrote the novel *Primary Colors*. He quite effortlessly combines quotes and summaries he's pulled from other articles with his own interviews, and his personal writing style is more like a clever columnist than a studied or neutral observer.

ASSIGNMENT

This is your most open-ended assignment. Try to find a discussion topic you think you can advance, or shed new light on. Your thinking won't be completely original—after all, you'll be quoting expert sources and data that others already have gathered. Use the essays discussed in this chapter as models: Each explores new areas of debates over Hiroshima, slavery, and the environment, respectively. If it helps to think "research paper," that's OK, but make your story readable. Even though the essays here are authoritative (not beyond reproach; not indisputable; not conclusive; but authoritative nevertheless), each is highly readable. You don't see any sentences beginning, "Research has shown … ." Nor do the authors send you running to the dictionary very often.

Shoot for 1,000 words or so.

8

Point of View

A surgeon I know once said there was no such thing as sterility.

"So why scrub before an operation?" I asked.

"To reduce the risk of infection, of course," he replied.

That's the argument about objectivity in a nutshell, too. Perhaps there is no such thing as pure objectivity, but we try to be objective to reduce the risk of bias, error, favoritism, skullduggery, whatever.

The debate on objectivity in the media is as old as the hills, but it really went haywire in the 1960s, with Vietnam, the civil rights movement, sexual liberation, and other topics dominating the news. These were all moral issues, and reporters, like many other citizens, wanted to take a stand. Being neutral, detached, objective wouldn't do.

And so developed a new journalism called, in fact, the New Journalism. Reporters put themselves in the story—no use pretending a reporter isn't actually asking the questions that prompts the quotes, or pretending that one side isn't more right or just than the other! The New Journalists, and many reporters after them who hadn't even known the roots of this movement, made the kind of judgments on events and personalities that previously were the province of editorial writers or authors with signed columns. The line between "news" and "opinion" became very blurred.

Here's what I think is really going on. I was a philosophy major in college and studied the English writer G. E. Moore. Instead of talking about objectivity and subjectivity he divided statements into "normative" and "descriptive" (Moore, 1903).

You shouldn't kill; you shouldn't do drugs; eat your vegetables; and get 8 hours of sleep: these are all examples of normative statements, what you would think of as statements about what is right and wrong, and what one ought and ought not do.

On the other hand, consider these statements: Pete Rose was banned from baseball for gambling; John F. Kennedy was assassinated in Dallas on November 22, 1963; a fetus is viable by the third trimester. These are all descriptive statements, what you'd think of as statements of fact.

What I think all New Journalists, advocacy journalists, and subjective journalists really mean to do is to make normative statements in their writing—to say what is right and wrong, and to tell the reader what he or she should be doing. In G. E. Moore's terms, they want to do normative writing, not descriptive writing.

But you still have to support any statement with facts and logic; you have to offer evidence, face scrutiny, and modify your position, or abandon it altogether, when a weakness is exposed. Taking a stand and writing normative statements in no way absolves you from doing the same kind of hard, serious journalism as those who stick with descriptive statements. If you understand this, then the debate over "objective" versus "subjective" becomes less significant.

I've decided to call this chapter Point of View, although I could have called it advocacy journalism. It's journalism with a cause. And the reporter is taking sides! You'll note in the following anti-capital-punishment story that, for the most part, only research that tends to undermine the notion of capital punishment's effectiveness in deterring crime is presented, and the lengthy profile of a leading anti-capital-punishment advocate is largely positive. People who still support capital punishment? They're likely to be dunderheads or politicians on the make. But the author in the following story does not glorify murderers or trivialize what they have done: The murderers on death row in this story are never sympathetic characters; their crimes are never forgotten.

Why have I included this story, though? If you recall from the Introduction, I said there are some tales so terrible—such as the genocide in Cambodia in the 1970s, for example—that I would expect you to point fingers, raise a hew and cry, and lead the people in protest.

Not all issues are so clear-cut, yet we do have people taking sides, staking out the moral high ground, and contradicting others who think that God and right are on *their* side. The issue of capital punishment is a case in point. I've included "A Quiet Voice Against the Death Penalty" because it is a good story, well-written and well-researched (though largely one-sided), but above all, because it is representative of the breed.

Another reason: The story comes from the pages of the *Phoenix New Times*, one of the grand-daddies of the New Journalism (and what also was called the Alternative Press, if you want to warehouse some more newspaper trivia). Many of you reading this text, if you want to leapfrog past the ubiquitous 12-inch traffic fatality stories you might have to do for your hometown daily newspaper on your first job out of school, and if you want to go beyond the fluff often thrown at you on the features desk ("Oh, we must do a story on the Volunteer of the Year at next month's United Way fund-raiser!"), will in fact seek employment at a paper like the *Phoenix New Times*, or the Boston *Free Paper*, or the Chicago *Reader*, where I freelanced in the mid-1970s.

~·≈·~

A Quiet Voice Against the Death Penalty: Amnesty International's Dr. Daniel Georges-Abeyie coolly argues the case against the punishment in our hang-'em-high state.*
by Michael Kiefer

Arizona is a hang-'em-high state, and its political leaders are death-penalty poster boys.

Gov. Fife Symington publicly blasted the courts for granting a stay of execution. Sheriff Joe Arpaio commended a journalist who witnessed a lethal injection for coming "to see what we do to murderers." Attorney General Grant Woods, a onetime defense attorney in capital cases, lobbied for federal legislation to limit the time-consuming legal obstacles between conviction and execution; then-senator Bob Dole lauded him for his efforts and President Clinton signed the bill into law.

Capital punishment in America is synonymous with law and order, and no politician who wants to be reelected will speak out against it.

Arizona has put six men to death since 1992, one in the gas chamber and the others by lethal injection, and the state plans another execution before the end of the year. Each time, the state clemency board, a prisoner's last chance of a stay or reprieve, has conducted its death-sentence hearings with unyielding adherence to the guilty verdicts.

And each of the six times the clemency board convened to decide if a man should live or die, telephones started ringing, and the anti-death-penalty forces mobilized to testify on behalf of a violent stranger and to stand vigil outside the state prison in Florence where the hearings and the executions took place.

Each side has Biblical passages to justify its stand: "An eye for an eye"; "Turn the other cheek"; "Thou shalt not kill"; "Whosoever sheds the blood of man, by man so shall his blood be shed."

The concept of punishing a crime with a like act is called lex talion.

"The only lex talion in jurisprudence is capital punishment," says Dr. Daniel Georges-Abeyie. "We don't rape rapists. We don't sodomize sodomists. We don't burn down the homes of arsonists. We don't steal from those who steal. It doesn't make any sense here either."

Dr. Georges-Abeyie (pronounced "Ah-bay-yee") is a world expert and walking encyclopedia on capital punishment, a professor of ad-

*From "A Quiet Voice Against the Death Penalty: Amnesty International's Dr. Daniel Georges-Abeyie coolly argues the case against the punishment in our hang-'em-high state." by M. Kiefer. Copyright © 1996, New Times Inc. Reprinted by permission.

ministration of justice at Arizona State University West. He is Arizona State coordinator for Amnesty International's program to abolish the death penalty, and because of his cool and reasoned manner, his ability to maintain a low and level tone in an argument that raises voices and blood pressures, he has become AI's point man in the western United States.

He is a man of striking presence, as dark and distant as an eclipse, precisely dressed, tautly academic and formal, with a locked-on gaze and gentle voice.

He has black belts in three different martial arts, and he wears that training as a thin veneer of self-control and serenity over a tense and passionate core. He's seen violence: He grew up in the South Bronx in the 1960s when it burned to the ground. Two of his older brothers were murdered, "one by poison and one by the knife," he says. But he won't say how or why, and offers only that their killers were never brought to justice. "My parents would not want me to talk about it," he says to end the line of questioning.

In March, Amnesty International sent Georges-Abeyie to Alaska to lobby state legislators against putting a capital punishment referendum on the ballot.

"There just weren't any questions he couldn't answer," says Barbara Hood, an Alaskan death-penalty abolitionist. The bill never made it out of committee.

In September, AI sent Georges-Abeyie to Oregon to address the media on that state's first execution in 34 years.

"He was the most remorseless killer I have ever seen," says Georges-Abayie, but he lobbied on his behalf anyway.

Twice this summer he delivered detailed legal analyses before the Arizona State Clemency Board, hoping to give the board members reason to grant a reprieve or a stay of execution to two brutal murderers.

Arizona is a predominantly white, conservative and anti-intellectual state, and Georges-Abeyie is a black, East Coast intellectual, defending a cause that is dismissed as liberal. So, if the board members don't recall Georges-Abeyie by name, they remember his face and his well-researched arguments.

Amnesty International, of course, is looked upon in this country as some vaguely left-wing collection of liberals fretting about political prisoners in places like Chile and China.

"Amnesty is not a political rights organization, we're not a civil rights organization," says Georges-Abeyie. "We're a human rights organization. There are certain rights that cannot be taken away and cannot be given up. They are your rights simply because you are Homo sapiens. And we defend those rights regardless of the political organization of the nation state."

Though AI has 6,000 members in Arizona, until recently it has not been a dominant force in the death-penalty-abolition movement in Arizona. The tenured protest groups, Middle Ground in Phoenix,

SOL:PAE (Sanctity of Life: People Against Execution) in Tucson, and the Catholic Church, frequently approach the topic from an emotional level, as a question of prisoner needs and rights. Before the last execution, for example, the Catholic Church and the prisoner rights groups lobbied to allow a condemned man's girlfriend to visit him in his last days.

"Daniel said that Amnesty International did not do that," says Ann Nichols of SOL:PAE. "He said, 'We conserve our energies for publicizing the death penalty, for the specific facts of the case that might make people believe that this shouldn't happen.'"

Amnesty International's approach is intellectual and coldly informational, bringing a voluminous library of research and resources and a global perspective to the local protest movement. It can cite studies that suggest the death penalty is prohibitively expensive and is practiced at the expense of budgets that could put more cops on the street. One such study says the U.S. spent $82 million on capital cases in 1993 alone; in California, capital cases have threatened to bankrupt county governments.

"It costs five to six times more to try a capital case than a noncapital murder case," says Georges-Abeyie. "Then it costs anywhere from two to five times more to execute a person than to incarcerate a person for 40 years to life at the highest levels of security."

Other studies have shown that the death penalty does not serve as a deterrent to murder because states with active death-penalty statutes have the same or higher homicide rates than states without them.

"It's as if you went to a physician and said, 'Give me the most expensive, ineffective prescription you have,'" says Georges-Abeyie.

A 1993 report of the U.S. House of Representatives judiciary committee found 48 men who were sent to death row and later found to be innocent. A recent U.S. Supreme Court decision, however, ruled that a convicted man could be put to death despite new evidence indicating innocence, so long as due process was followed during his trials.

In the more liberal 1970s, the Supreme Court threw out state death-penalty statutes because they verged on cruel and unusual punishment. As eyewitness accounts bear out, the electric chair, the gas chamber and lethal injection are not always efficient, instantaneous and painless forms of euthanasia.

"Amnesty is not opposed to punishment," says Georges-Abeyie. "We are not opposed to safety. We believe an offender should be punished. The issue is punishment without torture and abuse."

Furthermore, the 1970s courts noted that the death penalty was applied "capriciously." If the political makeup of the Supreme Court has changed enough in the past 30 years to cast those decisions aside, the capriciousness of imposing the death penalty, arguably, has not. In cases where more than one person committed the murder, usually only one is sentenced to death while the others turn state's evidence and receive lesser sentences. According to AI statistics, of 20,000 homicides, only 250 resulted in death penalties.

Daniel Georges-Abeyie has met monstrous murderers, men who buried women in the woods and then returned repeatedly to dig them up and rape the decomposing corpse. He knows of a man who killed women by ripping off breasts with his bare hands, another who carried severed genitalia in a plastic baggy. They did not go to the gas chamber.

"The point I'm trying to make is that the worst of our offenders, the most violent people, don't go to death row," he says, his soft voice never breaking cadence. "The social outcasts go to death row. The homosexuals and bisexuals go to death row. Nonwhites who kill whites go to death row. People with incompetent counsel go to death row. Persons with IQs below 80 go to death row.

"I could go on and on."

Daniel Georges-Abeyie so resembles the legendary Indian spiritual and political leader Mohandas Gandhi—if Gandhi had been buff, that is—that his friends call him "Gandhi." But few people seem to know him intimately. There is genuine warmth beneath his stern exterior, but he seldom reveals much of his past. He has fathered four children from two failed marriages, but he refuses to talk about them.

Instead, he seems to drive himself like a man trying to evade his memories. He escapes most weekends on trips with a Valley hiking club, of which he is president. Every evening he works his body for an hour and a half at a Scottsdale health club. He claims that he does 1,000 push-ups and 1,200 crunches every day.

He leads a martial-arts club at ASU West and gives private lessons in hapkido, a Korean street-fighting art that is at once beautiful and brutal. Hapkido is an art well-suited to Georges-Abeyie's temperament: It has graceful flowing motions designed to break bones contrasted with a strong intellectual abhorrence of violence and a vow to exhibit self-control even in the face of death.

"If I had not been in martial arts, I think that I would be in prison or dead," Georges-Abeyie says. "Everyone around me in my world in the South Bronx went to prison or went insane from drug use or alcohol or they died. I know at least eight men who were sentenced to death. I grew up with them. They were my cohorts."

Daniel Georges-Abeyie was born in New York City in 1948. His mother was a U.S. citizen, a Sea Islander, as the Gulla-speaking folk from the islands off the coasts of South Carolina and Georgia are called. His father was from Tortola, an island in the British West Indies, east of Puerto Rico. Both parents were descended from escaped slaves. "Georges" presumably was the name of the plantation that the father's ancestor had escaped from.

"'Abeyie' means 'return when the time is right,'" Georges-Abeyie says. "It's a Fanti name, from Ghana. The Fantis have a tradition that when a major life event occurs, the name changes."

Georges-Abeyie's mother wanted her children to be born in the U.S., but the family returned to Tortola shortly after Daniel's birth.

Georges-Abeyie spent the first five years of his life in an island paradise, but, as his grandfather told him, "You can't eat sea and sand," so the family moved back to New York, and Daniel's father became a New York Transit Authority police officer.

The family lived in a West Indian enclave in the South Bronx, and Georges-Abeyie remembers seeing vast firestorms from the windows of the family apartment as buildings were burned in rage or for insurance money. He remembers hearing rats moving inside the walls of the apartment and going to sleep with cotton in his ears to keep the roaches out.

"My father would take us every week on a car trip," he recalls. "He would take us downtown to see where the whites and the wealthy lived so that we could see the dramatic differences between the two worlds. He was telling us that we didn't have to live like this, that you didn't have to be an animal."

His mother would go to the A&P each week to get a new volume of Funk & Wagnall's encyclopedia and gather the children in the kitchen so that they could all take turns reading and playing games with the words on the page.

The African Americans in the neighborhood looked down on West Indians, calling their diet of plantains and assava and rice and mangoes "monkey food."

"Also, we were derided because we had an education orientation instead of a sports orientation," Georges-Abeyie remembers.

Anyone who didn't participate in sports was suspected of being a sissy or worse. For survival, Georges-Abeyie's uncles schooled him in the African-originated martial arts of the islands, usually called Capoeira, but which they called, simply, kickin' butt. The toughs in the neighborhood thought it was dirty fighting because it used kicks and sticks and razors, but it kept them at bay. Georges-Abeyie began studying jujitsu and boxing when he was 12, kempo karate as a young man, and finally hapkido when he was in his 20s. Because he could fight viciously, Georges-Abeyie was afforded respect on the mean streets.

He had three brothers and two sisters. His two oldest brothers were killed in separate incidents some years apart in South Carolina. "I would just attribute it to greed and jealousy," he says. Neither killer was captured or tried.

"You can kill blacks with impunity," he says.

Tortolan pride, he says, is sometimes excessive, and so he will not talk about the murders except in the abstract.

"The immediate reaction is always the same for a victim's family survivors," he says, "anger and rage. I would have liked to have seen these persons apprehended, tried and executed. But soon after, I opposed that. I would rather see them in prison for life, to take their freedom forever, not their ability to breathe and eat."

Striking out in fear or rage is animal behavior, a murderous but irrational trait we inherited from our unreasoning monkey ancestors.

"Some see homicide as a willful act of evil," Georges-Abeyie continues, "and I don't think that's the case with every individual. There are forces that are psychological and social and biological that are so powerful that they throw people toward certain behaviors."

Georges-Abeyie went to public schools in New York, and did well enough to get a scholarship to Hope College in Holland, Michigan. He studied for his master's degree in sociology at the University of Connecticut and a Ph.D. in urban, social and political geography at Syracuse University. Throughout his university days, he threw himself into civil rights and social justice student activism. Then he went on the academic fast track. By age 23, he was teaching at prestigious Johns Hopkins University, and he bounced through appointments at the University of Texas at Arlington, Penn State University and California State University at Bakersfield, and finally at Florida State University, where he was an associate dean.

Then in 1992 he was invited to teach at ASU West. Because the university requires its faculty members to participate in community service, he became adviser to the student chapter of Amnesty International—he had, after all, been an AI member since the mid-'60s. The assignment fit his only deeply held philosophical beliefs.

Two years later, at a regional meeting in San Francisco, Cossette Thompson, the western regional director of Amnesty International, couldn't help but recognize the impassioned authority with which George-Abeyie spoke about the death penalty. She appointed him to the western regional planning commission, a panel of 14 that sets agendas for AI, and made him Arizona state coordinator for death-penalty abolition.

Last spring, Ann Nichols of SOL:PAE, the Tucson-based anti-death-penalty organization, announced that she wanted to start a state coalition against the death penalty. Georges-Abeyie immediately responded.

"He became very active right away in helping us think through how to start the coalition, what were some of the issues we wanted to address in developing a statement of purpose that could gather people around without excluding any," says Nichols.

Amnesty International's Cossette Thompson recalls that just hours after the Berlin Wall came down in 1989, she received a phone call asking if the office would stay open.

"It was very symbolic of the prevailing perception that the major problems are only happening in countries on the other side of the globe," she says.

And earlier this year, when a condemned man was executed by firing squad in Utah, Thompson's phone lines burned with calls from journalists in other countries who were astounded that such a thing could happen in the bastion of freedom.

The United States is the only Western industrial nation that still has and uses its death penalty. No western European nations have death penalties for civilian crimes. And in the Western Hemisphere besides the U.S., only Chile, Cuba, Guatemala, Guyana and the Caribbean island nations still execute their citizens.

Despite United Nations covenants to the contrary, the United States will execute prisoners who are mentally retarded or suffering from brain damage, and we are one of just six nations worldwide—Nigeria, Pakistan, Saudi Arabia, Iran and Iraq are the others—that execute persons for crimes they committed before they were 18 years old.

Nichols of SOL:PAE hopes that the Arizona State Legislature will consider bills in the next session to stop both practices. She expects that her husband, Andy Nichols, a state representative from Tucson, will co-sponsor the bills, but she admits, "If we don't have a Republican co-sponsor, we're not going to get a hearing."

There are approximately 3,100 men and women on death row in the 38 U.S. states that still impose death penalties. California, Texas and Florida have the most capital prisoners; Arizona, though the nation's 24th largest state, has the tenth largest death-row population, with 120 men and one woman.

Arizona hanged its murderers until 1931. That year an obese woman who had been convicted for killing a chicken farmer stood, noosed, on the gallows, and when the trapdoor opened beneath her, the weight of her body falling pulled her head right off her neck. Because of that horror, the state built a gas chamber, which it used until 1963 and then—as the nation wrestled with the death penalty in state and federal courts—did not use it again until 1992, and then only once before switching to lethal injection.

Arizona judges still imposed the death penalty, but its legality hung in the balance for nearly two decades.

A 1972 U.S. Supreme Court ruling struck down all state death penalties for being capricious and erratic in their imposition. The Arizona law was rewritten in 1973 but was not used. The Supreme Court reinstated the death penalty in 1976, and a year later, Gary Gilmore faced a firing squad in Utah, the first person executed in a decade.

But the legal challenges had not ended, and the Supreme Court and the U.S. district courts continued to strike down state statutes as late as 1990. The current law calls for the death penalty for first-degree murder, that is, premeditated murder, when there are aggravating factors in the commission of the crime, such as rape or brutality or child molestation or other felonies. The sentence can be mitigated, however, by such things as the murderer's mental health and mental state at the time of the crime.

In March 1992, the state of Arizona put a convict named Don Harding in the gas chamber. It took more than 10 minutes for him to die. Horrified witnesses watched him choke and strain and moan in pain. The next year, the state began to kill by administering a lethal injection. Five men have been put to death since then, including two in 1996.

The first man to die this year, Daren Lee Bolton, refused any legal help on his behalf, choosing instead to die without putting up a fight. Daniel George-Abeyie spoke on his behalf anyway at his 45-minute-long hearing. But on June 19, Bolton was put to death.

On August 21, the clemency board met again to determine if there was any reason not to send a monster named Luis Mata to the death house.

Mata was one of three men who was implicated in the brutal 1977 murder of Debra Lopez. Mata and his brother Alonzo and a third man had been drinking with Lopez at their apartment, and when the woman got up to leave, Mata grabbed her by the hair and told her that they were going to rape her.

The men beat her until she passed out and, allegedly, while Luis Mata was raping her, she regained consciousness. She struggled and the two fell off the bed. Luis beat her head against the floor.

Luis Mata and his brother then carried her to their car and drove her out to the desert, where Luis slit her throat with an onion knife, cutting so deep that he severed her trachea and nearly decapitated her. Then they left her body by the side of the road.

They were caught immediately. The third man turned state's evidence against the Mata brothers; Alonzo was sentenced to life in prison and Luis was sentenced to death.

Capital punishment, however, requires a long string of appeals, some of them automatic, that are supposed to safeguard against executing innocent people. Mata's case raised eyebrows because the presiding judge, Stanley Goodfarb, was already under scrutiny for his continued use of ethnic slurs in the court; during Mata's case, he had referred to illegal Mexicans as "wetbacks." Furthermore, it had come to light that Luis Mata had suffered brain damage in an accident as a child. As an adult, he had an IQ of 64, virtually mentally retarded, which could have been a mitigating factor if it had come up during his original trial. In July 1995, Mata was granted a stay of execution by the courts so that those matters could be addressed.

Governor Symington expressed his outrage. Attorney General Woods worked to ensure that such stays couldn't continue.

"Those on death row who were counting on delays of ten years will find that, in two years, they will be executed," he told the media.

Time ran out for Luis Mata. His execution was set for 12:05 a.m. on August 22; the clemency board hearing started at 8 a.m. the morning before at the state prison in Florence.

The Arizona Board of Executive Clemency has seven members, all of them appointed by Governor Fife Symington. Their job in

death-penalty cases is to consider any last issues raised before the
convict is put to death. Then they can recommend that the governor
grant a temporary stay of execution or a reprieve. Neither of those sce-
narios has happened in the six capital cases brought before them
since the executions resumed in 1992. And in only one instance was
there anything less than a unanimous decision to execute; Mata's earlier stay had come from the courts.

Mata's lawyers raised a number of points, including his diminished
intelligence. They screened videotaped testimony from the prosecutor who originally tried the case, and he confessed that had he known
about Mata's mental capacity, he may not have recommended the
death penalty.

Daniel Georges-Abeyie addressed the board on behalf of Amnesty International and the Coalition of Arizonans to Abolish the
Death Penalty, not to forgive Mata his sins, but to ask that he be sent
to prison forever.

Georges-Abeyie admits that he is personally repulsed by the brutality of Mata's crime, and he began his speech by expressing his con-
dolences to the family before he stated his philosophical case.

"I believe, as Amnesty believes, that the taking of a life is the most
basic violation of the most basic human right, the right to life," he says
now. "The board knows that I will plead Eighth Amendment, that is
cruel and unusual punishment. They know that I will plead the Fifth
and Sixth amendments which protect due process issues associated
with the case. And they know I will try to point out any errors by the
prosecution."

On Mata's behalf, Georges-Abeyie presented "Sixteen points of
law," he says, along with unmentioned medical evidence suggesting
that Mata may not have actually raped Lopez.

The clemency board tapped feet and sat impatiently through his
talk. Witnesses claimed that at least two of the board members
seemed to be sleeping, one of them behind dark glasses.

"He puts on a very good presentation," says Duane Belcher, chairman of the clemency board, of Georges-Abeyie's efforts. "Obviously,
he has an agenda and he has a feeling about capital punishment and
the agency he represents. He obviously has presented to the board
information for serious thought, and especially when it comes to a situation where the board is going to make a recommendation of sparing or not sparing an individual that's getting ready to be executed."

"It was an effective presentation," concurs Mata's lawyer, John
Stookey. "The bottom line is that the clemency board wasn't going to
be convinced by anybody."

After a full day's hearings, the board had found no compelling reasons to stop the execution.

Shortly before the next morning, after giving up hope that any court
would grant a stay of execution, as Mata mouthed the words to the
Lord's Prayer, he was put to death.

Daniel Georges-Abeyie was outside the prison at the candlelight vigil that forms each time a man is executed, not just to protest the death penalty, but also to provide support for the family of the condemned man.

"We don't want someone executed in silence," George-Abeyie says. "We don't want someone executed without the public knowing."

But it was nothing more than a symbolic and frustrated gesture. Georges-Abeyie had decided not to bother with any more clemency board hearings.

"We are not going to win the battle through the courts," Georges-Abeyie says sadly. "We are not going to win the battle through the reprieve and commutation hearings. We must win the battle by educating people and winning hearts and minds. We must pass legislation. Our goal is to abolish the death penalty through legislation."

He went home crushed and exhausted.

Then, a week later, Amnesty International called and asked if he could fly to Portland, Oregon, to speak out against a pending execution there.

Dr. Daniel Georges-Abeyie packed his bag and went.

Dr. Georges-Abeyie is a saint, and capital punishment is inhumane. What else could you conclude after reading this story?

Well, it's not quite that simple here. This story definitely argues against capital punishment, yet it is not altogether one-sided or dogmatic. There are plenty of interesting, compelling, but easy to follow statistics offered which challenge the notion that capital punishment reduces crime, or even that it saves taxpayers' money. I would have liked a little more *attribution* for some of the studies alluded to in the story, but it's been an unfortunate trend in recent years not to bother the reader with such quaint details as the source of the data.

The author helps make his case via presentation of the data (usually as cited by Dr. Georges-Abeyie), but also in the veritable profile of Dr. Georges-Abeyie, which serves to reinforce the strength of the anti-capital-punishment sentiment because George-Abeyie is a heroic and mysteriously appealing figure.

Nevertheless, the author of this piece mercifully avoids telling us that every convict on death row must have been a child sex abuse victim himself, or a baby born to a crack cocaine-addicted mother, or that his or her criminality was directly predicated on a poor socioeconomic status.

No—these convicts are terrible people who did terrible things and ruined the lives of families like yours and mine. Note that the author is being just as judgmental and opinionated in this regard as he is in arguing that capital punishment is no good. But at least he's making judgments both ways, which has the advantage of separating the issues of "detachment" and "objectivity" from that of integrity and intellectual honesty. The author is not detached; he is apparently intellectually honest.

This is a fine example of what I'm calling "point of view" or, if you will, advocacy journalism.

Here's how the story is organized:

Part I.   Arizona politicians are on a killing frenzy.
Part II.   Dr. Georges-Abeyie wants to put an end to that killing.
Part II-A.   Dr. Georges-Abeyie is quite an interesting person.
Part III.   The facts are on the side of the anti-capital-punishment camp.
Part IV.   A lengthy aside on Dr. Georges-Abeyie's life (this might have been trimmed in some newspapers, or else it would have been broken out as a sidebar).
Part V.   Recent history of capital punishment decisions in America, but mostly as they affect Arizona. (This part really goes back to substantiating the rather brutal claims the author made in Part I.)
Part VI.   The Luis Mata case, which finally illustrates just what it is Dr. Georges-Abeyie really does when he argues against the death penalty.

I have no objection to Michael Kiefer's organization, but I must note that many traditional editors would suggest beginning with the Mata case, especially if it were still current (this would be your news peg, in effect). Then, one could get into the arguments about capital punishment, both pro and con, and perhaps have included some biographical material on this mysterious outsider, Dr. Georges-Abeyie. Finally, you would have finished with the outcome of the Mata appeal. Such an organization of material is the "sandwich" we learned about in an earlier chapter. Your lead and ending are essentially about the same matter, and everything in between is the meat of the story or, in the case of this story, context and background. There would have been nothing wrong with this kind of organization, but it's not what the author did.

I think the measure of success for a story like this is whether it changed your mind on anything. I found the writing to be pretty persuasive; I learned some things about the failures of capital punishment I hadn't known before, and I was relieved that murderers weren't painted as perpetual victims.

Also, I like passionate writing. Realistically, writers are only going to be passionate about issues and causes they believe in. If you see the journalist's role as opinion molder and shaper, and not just as some glorified stenographer, then this type of writing, which I have called point of view, is for you.

Nevertheless, I don't think much one-sided writing succeeds, except for people who already "believe." Preaching to the choir, as the old saying goes, isn't worth very much.

I think one-sided reporting doesn't work because, eventually, people will learn of the other side. Perhaps another reporter will discover that "studies" showing the death penalty doesn't reduce the murder rate are really comparing apples and oranges: The death penalty may be enforced in states with higher crime rates to begin with, hence comparing death-penalty-states to non-death-penalty-states may be misleading. Plus, witness the failure of media in state-controlled societies such as the Soviet Union. The Communist Party ruled that land and controlled media for more than 70 years, but ultimately they couldn't convince their own people of the rightness of their brand of socialism.

But point of view and/or advocacy journalism have their place, just like the prosecution and defense in a criminal trial. We know each side is going to be one-sided; that's why the courts want to hear two sides of a case. Similarly, if you're a good reader and serious thinker, then it's fine to read one-sided pieces, as long as you seek out the other side or sides, as well.

ASSIGNMENT

You should have anticipated this assignment. Write a story defending the death penalty. I don't care what you personally think, either. Try to find a particularly nasty murder case in your area, or in the nearest big city to where you live or study. Interview family members of the victims; they may already have been quoted in spot news stories about the murder you're following up on.

Find studies that purport to show the effectiveness of the death penalty, too (there are studies that support every belief these days, which makes one suspicious of studies, of course). Interview tough prosecutors (and include sympathetic biographical details; this is comparable to what Kiefer did in honoring Georges-Abeyie). Talk about bringing the case to "closure"; talk about America's need for safer streets; see if murder rates increased during the period in which the death penalty was not enforced in the United States.

I don't care what kind of outline you follow in this assignment, although here's a simple one that will work:

I. Focus on a family or family member at the time of a sentencing hearing in a capital case, or at any stage of the appeal process.

II. Recapitulate the gory crime.

III. Provide statistics on the number of murders in this country; quote family members from other murder cases on how they feel or felt (you can get some of these quotes from other articles you'll research, but be sure to give proper attribution).

IV. Show how the sentencing and appeals process has been so subverted in recent years that the average person on death row has a longer life expectancy than the average person who is newly diagnosed with cancer (look it up; it's true).

V. Go back to the sentencing hearing, or the appeal in question, and report the conclusion. If the death penalty is overturned, so much the better for your story. It'll stir up emotions just that much more.

Alternatively, write a proactive, one-sided, advocacy type of story on any major social issue of the day—abortion, the Israeli-Palestinian conflict, affirmative action—but do it from the point of view that is opposite what you really believe.

For example, if you choose to tackle the Israeli-Palestinian conflict, you can begin your story either by focusing on a Palestinian refugee living in your community (maybe even attending college with you) and how his or her life has been disrupted by the conflict, then go back over historically important events in this conflict (which I consider one of the great train wrecks of history). Or, you can find an Israeli citizen (again, perhaps on your college campus) and talk about his or her hopes for peace, followed by memorable events from war and terrorism that disrupted his or her life. You can cite facts and figures and historic declarations and find expert sources to comment on the conflict as well, of course. You'll find that it's extremely easy to be one-sided, no matter which side you decide to support.

Real Feature Writing
Part III

9

The Lead

The purpose of the lead often is explained in terms of function: It is there to hook the reader, to get him or her to read the rest of the story.

That sounds much too much like a mechanical function: It's like the first stage of a three-stage rocket, the booster that is meant to get the missile off the platform before it is jettisoned and lost over the ocean forever, its work complete so the serious business of space travel can carry on high above.

Anyway, with modern newspaper design, it would be more true to say that it is the headline, or the headline together with the *deck*, that expanded headline which comes between the regular headline and actual text, that hooks the reader. A graphic designer, too, might say that it is proper layout and good artwork that hooks the reader.

I have a stockbroker friend who says, "The sell is everything," meaning the sales pitch and the ability to close a deal are more important than what is actually being sold. I'm not sure I'd ever want to buy securities from such a fellow, as I'll be the one stuck with the stock when he's counting his commissions. But the analogy works for stories. A lead, a headline, or a strong art package can always help sell a story … but is a story there? I'd like to recommend a more honest approach to lead writing.

First of all, the lead, by definition, is the first part of your story. It's usually short, from one paragraph to three or four, although there always must be room for exceptions. What the lead accomplishes, beyond merely hooking the reader, is help the reader understand what kind of story he or she is getting. I call this being "true to the story." The lead must be true to the story.

For example, if you're doing a feature on an incurable, inoperative form of brain cancer, and you begin your story by focusing on a patient at a local hospital, that patient better be central to the whole story, not just the lead. You cannot have a heartbreaking image of a dying person in your lead, then follow up with a dry, talky story filled with experts and statistics and lots of other stuff about the cancer, but not about the personal tragedy you introduced in the lead.

There's a corollary here, too, as it applies to writing style. I've seen reporters agonize over cleverly or colorfully written leads, only to fill the bulk of their stories with dull, robot-like prose, or soft adjectives and vague abstractions. I've been to workshops where the lead ("the almighty lead," a facilitator at another seminar cried out, but facetiously, for she knew what a crock an overwritten, overworked, overwrought lead really was) was emphasized almost to the exclusion of the rest of the story.

Consequently, I say again that the lead must be true to the story. Characters and concepts, but also style and tone introduced in the lead should be carried through the story; you must get the rest of your story up to the level of your brilliant lead, or your story isn't ready for publication yet.

I have a respectable writing text in my collection that identifies 12 or 13 different "types" of leads. Scary, isn't it? I don't want you to memorize or work from lists of approved leads, though. If every story is a little bit different, then every lead can be a little different from the next, as well.

Having said that, there are some fairly recognizable types. Master just a few and you will go far.

The perennial favorite is the anecdotal lead. An anecdote is just a little story. But first, a word of warning: Sociologists often speak negatively about "anecdotal evidence" as opposed to properly collected, scientific data. By anecdotal evidence they mean isolated events, incidents, or stories from which you can't really generalize in any scientific way. Although we journalists always act as if we *can* generalize from one person's experience to an entire class of similarly placed persons (the cancer victim; the war refugee; the lottery winner), social scientists know better. Maybe the anecdote is representative of a larger trend or class of people; maybe it isn't.

This is worth emphasizing: We feature writers pretend we can generalize from one person's example, or one anecdote, all the time. I just advised you to do exactly that at the top of this section when I said if you introduce a dying cancer patient in a story about cancer, he or she must remain important throughout your story.

In this regard, feature writing is a lot like political propaganda. Political propaganda, too, often focuses on one example, then seeks to rally support around a greater cause. Bigots follow the same pattern: You find one member of a hated group who perhaps has engaged in questionable behavior, then argue "they" are all like that.

Similarly, revolutionary groups like to have martyrs who were killed by the central authorities: The martyrdom "proves" that the central regime is corrupt.

Well, it's the writer's art we're teaching here, not social science or political science. As writers, we write anecdotal leads, even if I can't pretend they're the most intellectually or scientifically valid tools we have. I can argue they're effective, however.

But there is another sense in which learning from an anecdote is quite valid, completely apart from the idea of generalizability. It is in our ability to identify with the hero or heroine or victim in a well-told anecdote, just as we do in a well-told story. Think of literature, for example. A great novel about the tragedy of war might focus on a young soldier's experiences, and most readers will feel they've learned some universal truths about fear and suffering and loneliness and the "kill or be killed" world of real warfare.

We might read of a young explorer's desire to climb the highest mountain and share in his or her joy at the mountaintop, and feel that we, too, now know, if even for a fleeting moment, what it must have been like to be at the mountain top.

Put a soldier in a foxhole; put an explorer on a windy high ridge; put a patient in the cancer ward, or an Olympic athlete at the training camp at dawn, or a young writer at the mailbox when he gets his or her first acceptance letter, or a young teacher in front of the third grade class on his or her first day of teaching, or ... well, you get the picture by now. All these scenes, all these moments, likely would make for great anecdotes that could lead to stories on, respectively, military training and downsizing of the army; the agony and the ecstasy of mountain climbing; the war on cancer; the drive to be the world's best at the Olympics; the inner life of a would-be writer; and education today.

As long as your lead really is related to the theme of your story, and the person or persons in the anecdote are relevant to what happens in the rest of your story, your lead will work.

But keep it short (every year, the trend in journalism is for shorter leads that get to the point more quickly); do use active verbs and graphic images where appropriate; and make sure the point of the anecdote is clear right from the gun.

I'm going to show you three simple examples of the anecdotal lead, all from *The Wall Street Journal*, which virtually "owns" this format.

Example 1

> Janet Dresden, 50 pounds overweight, tried Weight Watchers, the Diet Center, the Stillman Diet, the Atkins Diet, raw juice fasts, an "applied kinesiologist's" high-fat diet and nearly every other diet she ever heard of. Nothing worked. She would lose 20 or 30 pounds and gain them right back. (Reprinted from Miler, M., "Fat Pharm," *Wall Street Journal*, July 20, 1994.)

One-paragraph-long, but we know what the story is about (why diets fail) and we can feel Ms. Dresden's frustration. Ms. Dresden reappears several times in the story—she does not disappear from the scene like a booster rocket sinking to the bottom of the ocean after it's been expended—but we learn many other things related to dieting in the remainder of the story as well, of course.

Example 2

Seattle resident Michael Rozek says he woke up one morning three years ago feeling "like people who drink too much and one day decide they've had enough." But his hangover wasn't from gin; it was from free-lance writing.

Mr. Rozek says he had sold some 2,000 articles to magazines ranging from Esquire to Physician's Sports Life, and the experience left him feeling "brutalized."

He was fed up with editors making changes to suit their biases, he says, and sick of seeing 1,500-word features compressed into captions. He was also tired of profiles of actors, politicians and "people who committed some kind of heinous crime." Too much of what was published in the magazines he wrote for was "smug, trivial and self-serving." (Reprinted from Selz, "Old-Style Journalism for Today's Turned-Off Reader," copyright © 1996, *The Wall Street Journal*.)

I almost stopped after the first paragraph and called that the lead, but the first three paragraphs make a nice, cohesive package.

But I think we know, from just three paragraphs, that Mr. Rozek (pronounced Ro-zak, we are told a little deeper in the story), is a reformer, a modern Jeremiah who's going to tell us what's wrong with journalism today from the inside out. It's almost like someone defecting from the former Soviet Union to expose the abuses there, after years of external criticism that was not always believed.

The lead, in other words, has told us who the central figure (or driver) in this story is, and what his issue (mission, really) is all about. This is another example of a simple, straightforward, successful anecdotal lead.

Example 3

COUNTRYSIDE, Ill.—On a recent Saturday afternoon in this Chicago suburb, car salesman Robert Williams spent three hours selling a 1991 Nissan Maxima. The final price, $18,800, was $3,100 below the sticker, but that still left $800 of gross profit.

Mr. Williams' cut? Twenty-five dollars. At this rate, he isn't likely to top the $16,000 he made last year selling cars. And out of those earnings, he paid $1,920 for his medical insurance. (Reprinted from Patterson, "Tough Business, copyright © 1992, *The Wall Street Journal*)

The pattern should be clear by now: One person, one story, one problem. The sale indicates how hard it is for Mr. Williams—and by extension, many car salesmen—to make a living; it also gives us an insight into the dog-eat-dog world of competitive auto sales.

In fact, the remainder of the story fulfills this promise nicely. We revisit Williams throughout the story, but meet other car salesmen, some more successful than others, and we hear from the car dealer's point of view as well (the story turns out to be fairly well balanced; not all stories are). Once again, the lead was true to the story.

Now, here's an example of an anecdotal lead I wrote in 1997 for a consumer medical story on refractive laser eye surgery.

> In the temperature-controlled "clean room" of a Northside medical office building, Dr. William Whitson and two assistants prepare to zap a patient's eye with a laser powerful enough to evaporate her cornea, yet precise enough to split molecules.
>
> It's called refractive laser eye surgery, and up to 1 million people have had the in-office, same-day procedure to correct their vision since the 1980s.
>
> On this early winter morning Linda Barbee will be the latest patient to say "good-bye glasses, hello world."

Three sentences; three paragraphs. The lead is really quite short, but look at all you've learned. You are "there" as Dr. Whitson prepares to zap Ms. Barbee; you learn that this high-tech procedure now is quite common; and you should be able to feel Ms. Barbee's anticipation and excitement at having this procedure.

Ms. Barbee reappears in the story twice: First, when she is interviewed immediately after the surgery, and deeper in the story, after a follow-up telephone interview was conducted to see what the results were a week after the procedure. The rest of the story cites other doctors and patients, has lots of facts about the surgery itself, and ends with a long list of caveats and warnings about risks involved with laser eye surgery.

There may be many variations of the anecdotal lead, but they all tell a little story that is relevant to the rest of the story to come.

The next type of lead you should perfect is the simple summary lead. A good summary lead is better than a bad version of any other type of lead you can write, especially overly long anecdotal leads, or overly florid descriptive leads, or inane mystery leads ("Which '50s-era television star hosted his own show for six years, launched the careers of some of your favorite comics, and was brought to you by the most popular brand of gasoline on the market?")

Fact is, you can never go wrong with a clearly written, to-the-point, accurate summary lead. For it has the great, great saving grace of at least telling your reader up-front, in no uncertain terms, without wasting his or her precious time, what the story is about. In that sense, a summary lead is much like the nut graf noted several times already in this book.

Here's a respectable summary lead from the Jan. 22, 1998 edition of *The New York Times*. As you can see the news peg is the 25th anniversary of the Roe v. Wade abortion decision.

> Twenty-five years after the Supreme Court recognized a constitutional right to abortion, tens of thousands of abortion opponents marched to the court today in somber protest, while abortion rights advocates pledged to fight any rollback. (Mitchell, 1988)

No persons are mentioned by name in the lead, although that is not verboten in a summary lead. We are not told in detail of an incident or anecdote. This lead succeeds not because it is artful, in other words, in other words, but because we know in the first sentences why the story is being written at this time, and how it's going to break down to two sides of the argument.

Summary leads most often are linked to news stories, of course. Some textbooks will use the term "news lead" in its place.

Here's a summary lead from an Associated Press article that's brightly written.

> Space shuttle Endeavour slid up to Mir and docked Saturday, bringing a fresh American astronaut to relieve a homesick David Wolf. (Dunn, 1998)

This is a good summary lead because it has some active verbs in it—"docked" and "slid"—and decent adjectives that give the right flavor to events—"fresh" and "homesick."

Here's a brighter example still of what you can do with a summary lead:

> Buffalo, N.Y.—Had the psychics been right, 1997 would have gone down in history as the year Mick Jagger became a member of Parliament and Walter Cronkite a critically acclaimed lounge singer. (Thompson, 1998)

This Associated Press story was appropriately titled, "Psychics strike out: No prediction for '97 came true." The story is all about psychic predictions made a year earlier. In a clever way we are told what the rest of the story confirms (and what the headline gave away, actually): The psychics don't know what they're talking about.

Now, here's a summary lead from a feature series on aging I wrote years ago.

> They are America's fastest-growing population group.
>
> Centenarians. People who were alive when President Benjamin Harrison was inaugurated and George Eastman improved his famous hand camera, the Kodak.

"These people are survivors," says Mary Jane Koch, a gerontologist at Indiana University-Purdue University at Indianapolis. "They've probably lived through the death of their spouse. Maybe their children." (Aamidor, 1980, p. D1)

I interviewed about 15 centenarians—people more than 100 years of age—for this three-part series, plus sidebars. What you have is the lead for the first story. Many of the people were delightful, sharp-witted, and eager. I thought of leading with an anecdote about one of the centenarians, but I felt the best way to put all of the centenarians under one umbrella was a summary lead. An anecdotal lead would have worked had I fewer old people to work with, and if I wasn't writing a series. But focusing on one person in the lead could have worked: I would only have needed to be very careful in my nut graf to state that so and so is a member of a class, "one of a growing number of centenarians."

I generally don't like quotes up high in my leads (not a rule, just a preference), but the quote from Mary Jane Koch really helps sum up what this story is about, so I used it. I think the lead, as written, although by no means brilliant, still is effective at making its point as to what the story and series to come are about.

One last note about this last lead: Some books admonish you not to use "one word" leads, as in my one word sentence, "Centenarians." Also, some authors don't like history or almanac lessons, stories that being with, "On this day in 1492 blah happened." Have I violated their rules? I wanted to make the point that much transpires over a 100-year period, and that these centenarians have seen a great deal.

Even if I broke the rules, my lead told the reader exactly what the series to come was about, and that's about all I ever ask of a summary lead.

The third type of lead often is called the descriptive lead, for reasons that will become obvious almost immediately. I include it not so much because I favor it, but because I want to issue the following warning: Handle With Care.

The descriptive lead is the most dangerous, seductive, and abused lead you will attempt (and I know you will attempt it). Everybody who loves to write, and wants to be a writer, not merely a reporter, thinks painting pretty pictures and writing beautiful prose and setting the scene is what it's all about.

I rarely attempt purely descriptive leads. But I get up there and take my cuts sometimes. The following is from a story on a missing link to Yellowstone National Park.

The little, leather-covered diary, about the size of a greeting card and as slim as a checkbook, lies on Lee Parsons' dining room table, its pages as fragile as dried leaves.

Parsons, an Indiana environmentalist and amateur historian, had tracked this diary since 1980. It was written in 1870, then lost to history for all those intervening years.

The diary, written in the hand of Henry Dana Washburn, chronicles the first official survey of that portion of the northern Rockies which was to become the nation's first national park, Yellowstone. (Aamidor, 1998a)

Gotcha! It's really a summary lead, though the first paragraph certainly is descriptive. In fact, most of the story is flush with descriptions of the park, and the animals and wilderness there, and even of the soldier and surveyor Washburn himself, so the lead is true to the spirit of the story in much the way I demanded for all leads at the beginning of this chapter.

But I don't think the first, highly descriptive paragraph would have worked unless I immediately got to the point of the story. Nobody is going to care for long about a little, leather-covered diary on somebody's dining room table.

The lesson here? Be descriptive, wax poetic, if you must. But get to the point of the story—quickly!

Here's a particularly evocative lead from Bill Shaw, a fellow reporter at *The Indianapolis Star* who formerly wrote for *People* magazine and other national media.

GUILFORD, Ind.—On Sept. 16, 1993, Bill and Thelma Jean Taylor were watching the late news in their farmhouse along the West Fork of Tanner's Creek when the fire department beeper squawked to life.

Bill, 66, a Miller Township volunteer firemen, threw on clothes, rushed out the door and saw fire in the night sky. He felt sick. The 118-year-old Guilford Covered Bridge, a local landmark and powerful emotional symbol to this tiny Dearborn County farming community, was engulfed in flames. (Shaw, 1997a, p. B1)

Can you picture this? Bill and Thelma in front of the old TV? Can you hear the beeper "squawking" to life?

Flames in the night sky? See them, too? The bridge is on fire; the bridge is on fire!

This is not only a highly descriptive and successful lead, but it's dynamic, not static. By that I mean the writer has described action; things are happening here, not just lying on a dining room table. The moral of the story? If you're going to describe things, describing action is better than painting pretty pictures.

Yet you will need a nut graf very soon to tell what this story is about, too. Is it a profile of Bill and Thelma? The story of losing and rebuilding a historic bridge? How a volunteer fire department operates? You can't really tell from this otherwise delectable descriptive lead.

Here's another descriptive lead, from the Associated Press.

PITKYARANTA, Russia (AP)—In the deepening dusk, a young man comes weaving up a snow-covered street.

It is a gloomy street of shambling wooden buildings long untouched by paint, of small windows and little light. As the man steps unsteadily out of the shadows, his face comes into focus: It is round, the hair pulled back into a pony tail, the mouth formed into a sneer.

A cigarette dangles from one hand. His breath smells of tobacco and alcohol. He gives his name as Andrei, his age as 30.

"I smoke," he says defiantly. "Smoking is not a problem for me. I always smoke when I drink."

He takes a short, hard drag and glares.

"Frankly speaking, I did not smoke for two months," he says. "Then I lost my job. Well, now I have nothing to do but drink and smoke."

Once a railroad worker, Andrei now sits home ... . (Landsberg, 1998)

So much description, this could be the opening scene in a novel. In fact, it's a long feature about economic dislocations and unemployment in the former Soviet Union. The lead is highly descriptive, but could also be considered an anecdotal lead, or even the beginning of a focus structure story about unemployment that focuses on one individual's misery throughout the entire story.

I don't know if I like the lead that much, though. Do you? It doesn't get to the point (the nut graf, in this case) until several paragraphs deeper in the story. Is the lead so colorful, so haunting, so dramatic, that most readers would have held on until that nut graf? I don't know. But this is a case in point of living dangerously as a writer. If you're going to attempt a great descriptive lead, it better be great.

Special Note: You may have heard that a journalist should never employ a "question lead." What is usually meant by this is the practice of beginning a story with a question for the sole purpose either of answering it in the very next sentence, or quoting someone immediately.

For example, one might begin a story badly this way:

What did Russian cosmonaut Yuri Kerensky say when he first set foot on Mars?

"This is one small step for a man, but one giant step for mankind."

With apologies to American astronaut Neil Armstrong, who said something like this when he set foot on the Moon in 1969, you can see that the question is superfluous and gratuitous here: We just don't need it to set up

the quote that follows. You could just as well create context for the quote
by acknowledging the historical event (man lands on Mars), then quoting
the source.

Here's another made-up example of a bad question lead:

When did World War II erupt?

It was on Sept. 1, 1939, when the German Army smashed through the Polish
frontier, unleashing a chain of events that saw 50 million young soldiers and
innocent civilians from all sides perish, and which caused untold trauma in
those who survived.

If it's important to your story to introduce the first day of World War II,
then by all means do so. You just don't need to waste time on a question before introducing the relevant fact or facts.

Having said this, there is at least one special case where a question lead
can be a superb tool, where it will serve as a veritable theme statement for
the entire story to come. This is when you are asking (or identifying) *what is
the problem*, and indicating to the reader that the rest of the story will seek to
explore said problem.

Here's how I used a question lead in a story on Sharon Aschen, a
49-year-old woman who was diagnosed with inoperable spinal cancer.

What would you do if you were told you had six months to live?

Sharon Aschen decided to call an ex-college roommate and five other friends
she hadn't seen in at least 20 years.

Then she held a party for them and more recent acquaintances, variously calling the get-together an "affirmation of life" and a "living funeral." (Aamidor,
1998b, p. J1)

The reason I began the story with a question was largely because I
wanted to involve the reader—to put "you" in the picture. But that single
question posed the most human of dilemmas we all face, namely our own
mortality. Having accomplished that, the story goes on to tell how Aschen
dealt with this crisis in her life.

And, a very last note on "quotation leads":

You may have been told not to use them, and that's generally good advice,
too. The reason not to use quotation leads is that the reader doesn't know who
the speaker is, and context for the quote has yet to be established.

Nevertheless, this is a rule that can be broken on occasion. John Camp, a
writer for the *St. Paul Pioneer-Press*, began a multi-part series on farming in
the Upper Midwest with a six-paragraph-long quote (Camp, 1985).

Most journalism instructors, and most section editors on most newspapers, would tell you never to do that. They would strike the quote, make

you change the lead, and begin to wonder aloud whether you really had what it takes to be a journalist.

But John Camp won the Pulitzer Prize for feature writing for his series on farming that began with a six-paragraph-long quote.

Although I generally would discourage you from using quotation leads, the argument about identifying the source or establishing context first is a bit of a red herring. With modern newspaper layout and graphics, and the use of magazine-style titles and "deck" headlines under the title, most readers will have some idea who the speaker is, and what he or she is talking about, even if you begin your story with a quote. Just don't do it often. I don't like quotation leads because they become a cheap trick that encourages laziness in reporters. Usually, you can do better than a quotation lead.

10

Observation
for Detail

Several years ago a student named Evelyn arrived for class at Indiana University in Bloomington: she looked particularly long-faced and forlorn. She took her seat at the big seminar table in our classroom just off the library at Ernie Pyle Hall, folded her arms and plopped her head down.

"What's wrong?" I asked her. It was completely uncharacteristic behavior for her.

She lifted her head and brushed back her hair and said something like this: "You know that assignment you gave us, to find a piece of writing with really good observation? Well, I found this article on Hurricane Hugo and it is so well written. I'm sad because I know I'll never be able to write that well."

Hugo hit Charleston, South Carolina, and environs in September, 1989; the article originally appeared in *The Miami Herald*, although Evelyn found it in a collection of "best writing."

I asked to see the story and as I scanned it I wanted to cry, too, for much the same reason Evelyn gave. The story was so rich in detail and observation—the eyes and ears of the reporter, David von Drehle, were so sharply focused and tuned—it was hard to imagine anything else ever written that put you, the reader, *there*, where the story was.

Let me just give you a few selections from the story, which was titled simply, "Shaken Survivors Witness Pure Fury":

> Sundown, and gray drains from the sky, leaving only black. The tension rises another notch. In the gloaming, the trees ball and buck in the rising winds ....

128

A thick steel flagpole, barely anything to it to resist the wind, is bent at a 60-degree angle. An ancient Pontiac, finned and weighty, has been shoved several feet into a Saab. A Chrysler New Yorker is deposited on the sidewalk....

The ground is thick with tree limbs and glass and aluminum and shingles and bits of plastic signs. Bits of Sheraton, bits of McDonald's.... (von Drehle, 1989, pp. 1, 2)

It's all observation. Ripping selections like this from the full original destroys the mounting tension as the author describes waiting for the worst, and finding it all to be much worse than he could ever have anticipated. Nevertheless, you see what Von Drehle sees; you feel his awe at the power of the hurricane.

And it's accomplished all through observation. The reader couldn't be there, but the writer was. He or she has to show what it (whatever it is) was like, in graphic detail.

Lots of people say, "You can't teach writing." I'm not sure what is meant by such a pessimistic injunction, but there certainly are some things about good writing you can teach.

Note the specific, concrete, tangible, palpable images the author gives the reader in this selection: the bent steel flagpole, the weighty ancient Pontiac, a gray sky turning black.

This is just a part of the original story, but the author consistently delivers concrete, tangible, palpable images, things that he—and anyone else with acute senses—could see and hear and feel. He was being very observant. And there are few adjectives or superlatives here, all of which are usually cheap tricks inadequate writers employ to pump up an otherwise flaccid story.

Here's a selection from a long Sunday magazine article (many newspapers formerly published Sunday magazines, but other than *Parade Magazine*, they're rare now) written in the 1960s. It's titled "The Hashbury Is the Capital of the Hippies." After you've read the selection I'll tell which newspaper originally carried it, and who wrote it. You may be surprised.

The best show in Haight Street is usually on the sidewalk in front of the Drog Store, a new coffee bar at the corner of Masonic Street. The Drog Store features an all-hippy review that runs day and night. The acts change sporadically, but nobody cares. There will always be at least one man with long hair and sunglasses playing a wooden pipe of some kind. He will be wearing either a Dracula cape, a long Buddhist robe, or a Sioux Indian costume. There will also be a hairy blond fellow wearing a Black Bart cowboy hat and a spangled jacket that originally belonged to a drum major in the 1949 Rose Bowl parade. He will be playing the bongo drums. Next to the drummer will be a dazed-looking girl wearing a blouse (but no bra) and a plastic mini-skirt, slapping her thighs to the rhythm of it all. (Thompson, 1967, p. 120)

This is all pretty graphic, even evocative. It was another of my Indiana University students who brought this article to my attention. I'd say the descriptions are less literally true than those sampled in the Hurricane Hugo story, but I could be wrong—the subject matter is different and that might explain the fancifulness in this latter selection.

In both cases, though, the writer is standing firm, aiming his eyes and ears and sensory power at the subject matter, and describing what he sees. That's observation.

The story originally appeared in *The New York Times*; it was written by a then-young freelance writer named Hunter S. Thompson.

Here's a selection from something I wrote several years ago; it's from a story based on my first visit to a NASCAR race. The setting is the night before the race at Michigan International Speedway in Brooklyn, Michigan.

The first rule is to remember where the portable toilets are located.

Five thousand camper vans, Winnebagos and converted old school buses, toting an estimated 25,000 men, women and children, squat willy-nilly on the dry brown grass of the speedway infield this hot June night, squeezed in as tightly as cattle in a box car.

They are here for the Miller Genuine Draft 400; here to see Dale and Rusty and Ricky and Ernie race so close you could jump a spark between their respective fenders; there to holler and drip sweat and chug more beer in 24 hours than the entire adult population of Milwaukee could in twice that time.

Small campfires and barbecues burn black holes in the grass everywhere; people boil water in pots hanging from wrought-iron metal strands or roast hot dogs and brats over the open flame, or just sit around in folding lawn chairs lapping up the evening.

Young men in their 20s, almost all white-skinned, bare-chested and beer-guzzling, stand and sway in the hazy, glowing night mist from the backs of pick-up trucks. The trucks wander aimlessly; they snake down a narrow, meandering blacktop road through the crowded, stifling infield.

Some of the men whoop and yell at passing women, egging them to remove their bikini or tube tops (most women here are wearing one or the other); one young man bends over and "moons" a gaggle of hecklers who watch the parade from the sidelines.

Some of them raise their fists and arch their backs and bellow the names of their favorite drivers toward the heavens.

"Earnhardt!" and "Rusty Wallace!" are the principal gods worshiped at this holy NASCAR shrine.

Behind the pick-ups, dozens of younger boys, junior clones of those in the trucks, wheel along on 20-inch BMX bicycles, weaving from side to side to keep their balance in the slow pace of traffic, or reach forward to try and catch a bumper in front of them … . (Aamidor, 1994a, p. J1)

A scene is being described above, but it is not static. People are moving, shouting, sweating; the evening mist and smoke are tactile, even palpable; perhaps you can smell the meats cooking over the open fires? You should be able to see the little kids on their little bikes trailing the pick-up trucks and reaching forward to grab the bumpers for a free pull. It's all descriptive writing based on keen observation, which is what you want to do.

Reminder: Describing action is actually easier, and more interesting, than describing static scenes. Describe people doing things; describe something that's happening. You might not run into a hurricane every day, but always look for the action, the little touch or quiver, the flexing muscle that evokes a real image.

Additional hint: Nouns are better than adjectives; verbs are better than adverbs. Yet you are not forbidden to use adjectives and adverbs; just don't use them to compensate for what is weak description to begin with.

Last hint: I don't like writing samples that contain evaluatives and superlatives (like "wonderful," "exciting," "best," "most," and so on), but not many concrete words. Such samples lack "thingness," which is what you should always come away with if you've done real observation and carefully noted the details along the way. Don't tell me about an elderly lady's "sunny disposition"; don't tell me about a young actor's "boyish good looks." *Show me* real lines on an aged person's face; *show me* the bounce in a frisky young horse's gait.

Also, active and colorful verbs are better than business-oriented or bureaucratic verbs. For example, you may "negotiate" a better price on that new car you're after, but "haggling" and "whittling down" the price is more colorful.

I once wrote about a 39-year-old Indianapolis radio personality who had double bypass heart surgery; his arteries were not only clogged, but "gummed up" as well.

11

Interview Techniques

The primary way we get information from sources has not changed since newspapers cost a penny a copy.

We ask questions; we interview people.

There are plenty of texts or guides available on "how to interview" and this short chapter cannot condense all the wisdom they contain. But here are some general guidelines and tips that will work for most of you.

Successful interviewing is a bit of a balancing act: You want to act professionally, but you need to be friendly, too. Some reporters work from a set of questions, but I'd suggest committing a few good questions to memory, then being flexible during the actual interview. You need to allow yourself follow-up questions, and the source may take you down unexpected roads. Don't be afraid to tag along with him or her.

The first thing is to read up on your subject (either on the person you're interviewing, if it's a profile, or the issue you're investigating) before the critical interview. It is very unprofessional to go into an interview unprepared. Imagine how you'd feel if you were being interviewed for your role in producing a school play, or in winning some national academic honor, and a reporter coming to do a story on you doesn't know the name of the play or the academic honor.

If you're doing a little profile of a famous author who has come to town or campus, for example, you should have no difficulty reading up on him or her. I've discussed databases and reference materials separately. But you could look up the author in reference works such as *Books in Print* or *Current Biography*, or even in *Who's Who*. Your newspaper library may have clips on the person; do a keyword search using a search engine on the Internet (the author may have his or her own web site). If worse comes to worst, the publisher or publicist for the author will have a short tip sheet or backgrounder for you to use (but use these things only as a starter; they're often not very good).

I interviewed syndicated political columnist William Raspberry when he appeared in Indianapolis in late 1997. Biographical information on him was surprisingly sparse. I knew Raspberry was represented by the Washington Post Writers' Group, so I got the number for that organization from the *Editor & Publisher Yearbook*, which every journalism library will have. The people at the writers' group actually had a better-than-average biography on file for Raspberry, and that served as a starting point for me to ask my own questions. (Don't ever take anything you read at face value if you can help it; confirm everything!)

Let me follow up on the Raspberry interview. Raspberry is an African American author born in Mississippi, educated in Indianapolis (he came north to live with his sister while attending college in Indianapolis), who has lived in Washington the last 35 years or so, where he has enjoyed his greatest success. He was visiting Indianapolis to speak at the Tuskegee Airmen Inc. National Convention (the Tuskegee Airmen were the first African-American combat pilots in World War II).

Besides the short biography from the Washington Post Writers' Group, Raspberry offered me a copy of his speech to read in advance of the interview. This was helpful because he could not give me much time in person. So, I read a little and knew a little before sitting down to ask my own questions.

We sat in a garden outside the upscale hotel where he spoke. It was a nice early fall day in Indianapolis, so why not? Comfort is one of the things you want to achieve in the interview setting.

I made a little small talk at first—How was your trip? How is your family? Who's going to win the next mayoral election in Washington?—before settling into the "real" interview. It's usually a good idea to put your subject at ease (and yourself) by beginning an interview with some soft questions that really won't have much to do with your story.

I used a reporter's notebook on this day, but I often use a tape recorder. Most interviewing texts I've seen advise against using a tape recorder; they say they're unreliable, and that they intimidate the source.

Hogwash! It's just a matter of personal preference. The fact is, tape recorders are highly reliable (as long as you change batteries and tapes often), and they're certainly more accurate than trying to keep up with someone who speaks fast. In my feature writing classes I always have one student interview another on a topic of mutual interest while the rest of the students take notes. Almost NEVER does any student take notes perfectly accurately. How do I know? I tape-record the interview and the students compare their notes to "the record" when I play back the tape.

Plus, technology is rapidly advancing in terms of voice recognition computer software. One company already makes a tape recorder that downloads directly to a computer with voice recognition software; the manufacturer currently claims 95% accuracy. That's not accurate enough for journalism, so I wouldn't use such a system yet. But when it gets up to 99% -plus accuracy I'll be the first in line to buy the equipment. As it is, some top newspapers require their reporters to tape-record all sensitive interviews, and the companies provide transcription (secretarial) services to change the tapes into neatly typed computer files, which is what you always want to work from when you are ready to write your story.

(Trying to write a good story from messy, handwritten notes you have to constantly flip through to find the information you want is nearly hopeless; transcribing your own handwritten notes onto computer pays dividends in accuracy, in finding facts and quotes faster, and in forcing you to read your notes at least one more time.)

The issue of "intimidating" a source by the presence of a tape recorder is a proverbial red herring, too. Just as many sources will look over your shoulder, or at your lap, to sneak a peak at what it is you're writing about them. The very act of taking notes often is disruptive; looking down as you write, instead of making eye contact with your source, is always uncomfortable.

The wise journalist uses a tape recorder whenever possible, but also takes partial notes for really important facts and quotes during the interview.

Another issue at the top of the list in interview texts is what kind of questions to ask. Generally, you do not want to ask questions that allow for simple yes or no answers. You want open-ended questions.

For example, don't ask William Raspberry, "Were you born in Okolona, Mississippi?" First, you should know the answer to that question before starting the interview. Second, he's just going to say, "Yes."

Rather, ask him, "How was it growing up in Okolona?"

Similarly, if you're interviewing a songwriter, ask questions such as, "What was your favorite song?" Or, "How did you come to write that tune? Was it a happy or sad time in your life?" These are all questions to get him or her going, to get a conversation going.

You'll see a chapter on the best use of quotes after this section, and I've discussed the importance of quotes periodically in previous chapters. It's worth reminding you that quotes are born of one method only—you ask questions, they answer. If you ask interesting, open-ended questions, you get interesting, quotable answers.

A couple of more points: You are the interviewer, not the interviewee. Even if you get a nice conversation going with the source, which is good, the source does NOT need to hear of your lengthy experiences or opinions on this and that topic of the day. You won't be writing about yourself in the story; you'll be writing about the source. This is a classic mistake that many beginning and even some veteran reporters make: They talk too much. Don't do this.

Also, be nonjudgmental. By this I mean do not show your disgust or anger or contempt at whatever it is your source is telling you. Maybe you're interviewing a hardened racist who's organizing a klan rally; maybe you're interviewing a crack cocaine dealer behind bars; maybe you're interviewing an abortion doctor or someone who shoots rifles at abortion clinics. There are all sorts of things out there that may affect you, and about which you may have strong feelings, but you must let the source speak. It's for the Jerry Springers of confrontational TV talk shows to express their views and feelings in real time, right on air, but that is not a journalistic model you're going to follow, even if you're doing research for an editorial or essay where you will take a position.

Another good tip about interviewing someone: Generally, when you are finished, ask the source if there is anything you failed to address, but on which he or she would like to comment. This shows respect and common courtesy; you may also get useful information you actually forgot to inquire about. By the same token, ask your source to refer you to other knowledgeable sources, either who are familiar with his or her background (if it's a profile) or familiar with the subject or controversy at hand (for other types of stories). You can get some really good new sources this way.

12

Best Use of Quotes

Most beginning journalists use either too many or too few quotes. The reason some over-quote is clear: It's just easier to sit at a terminal or typewriter, flip through pages of your notebook, and quote away.

The reason for not quoting enough is less clear, but often the problem is mechanical. By this I mean the reporter didn't take any full quotes in his or her notes, so he or she cannot quote anyone.

Each semester that I taught advanced writing I'd look for two volunteers from the class, one to ask questions on this or that topic, and the other to answer them. A few minutes later, I'd invite the rest of the class to ask questions, too. I always tape-recorded these sessions.

Afterward, I'd ask students to read back their notes. Half the students had recorded no quotes. They may have summarized this or that statement, or taken down a couple of figures, but they didn't quote interesting statements or complete sentences. Other students often got their quotes wrong—not major mistakes, perhaps, but real anomalies in what they wrote as compared to other students. I'd prove all this to my students by playing back the tape.

A good quote is like an inflection in a person's voice. Beyond the mere content, it can signal sadness, glee, coyness, rage, or self-doubt. Using quotes effectively falls squarely within the "show, don't tell" philosophy of good writing.

Here's a quote from a story on a 101-year-old woman who has lived her entire life in rural Indiana. The quote comes at a moment in the interview when the woman needs to rest for a bit. "Pardon my old-lady shoes. My feet hurt. I hate these shoes." (Shaw, 1998, p. J1)

This simple, single quote speaks volumes about the woman. You don't have to call her ornery or spunky; you don't have to say she's a tough old broad; you don't have to say she's down-to-earth. We can see it in the quote. The quote is from a profile of Ann Vollmer, written by Bill Shaw, whose writing you previously saw in the chapter on leads.

Later, in the same story, we are told that Vollmer keeps a loaded handgun near her bed. Then, she is quoted as saying, "I like a revolver. You can count on it."

Part of what makes the quote exciting is that the woman is, after all, 101. It blows away any stereotypes you might have of centenarians, if you'll pardon the pun. But the second sentence in the quote is the better part: "You can count on it." Would anyone doubt she means business after hearing her talk like this? I bet she has a steady hand when she fires her weapon, too (Shaw, 1998, J2).

Here's another provocative quote—the first quote in the story—from "A Quiet Voice Against the Death Penalty, " which you read in the chapter on point of view. I'll keep it in the context of the lead, where it appeared.

Arizona is a hang-'em-high state, and its political leaders are death-penalty poster boys.

Gov. Fife Symington publicly blasted the courts for granting a stay of execution. Sheriff Joe Arpaio commended a journalist who witnessed a lethal injection for coming "to see what we do to murderers."

The author wants to paint death penalty supporters as a blood-curdling lot. This single, partial quote does more than all the name-calling rhetoric or condemnations from secondary sources he could ever have employed.

Think back to the progress vs. historic preservation story in the chapter on pro and con. Remember the tough call on whether to demolish the attractive, but nearly vacant MaCo Building in Indianapolis in favor of a new drug store and parking lot? I still like the following quote from a neighborhood resident who supported new construction: "If Benjamin Harrison had slept there, it might be historic. But he not only didn't sleep there, he didn't even shop there."

It was just a homespun, down-to-earth, unpretentious thing that pegged the speaker as what we used to call a "regular guy."

Here's a string of quotes from the story about Sharon Aschen, the 49-year-old woman who was dying of spinal cancer, that I introduced in the chapter on leads. She and an aunt hosted an "affirmation of life" party, which also was called a "living funeral." Fifty people came to the party, but some refused.

Why? The dying woman explains in her own words:

"One relative said, 'What if you don't die in March? Won't you be embarrassed?'" Aschen recalled.

Another brusquely declined, telling her, "I'll come to the real funeral."

"Some people said they don't believe in this," Aschen added. "I'm still trying to understand what part they don't believe in. Camaraderie? Friendship? Affirming a life?" (Aamidor, 1998, p. J2)

The writer could have said something like this: *Some of Aschen's relatives and friends were unmoved by her imminent death, arguing it was inappropriate to have a celebration prior to her death, or otherwise making excuses for not attending.*

But such a paragraph or statement would have been vague, impersonal, and guilty of the "tell, don't show" school of journalism. Using three strong quotes in a row made the point much better; the reader could also sense Aschen's frustration and even outrage that some people did not approve of her affirmation of life party. (Yes, it's rarely the case that you will need to string quotes together like this in a story. But you know the old saying, "The proof of the pudding is in the tasting." These are short quotes and I think they work as a group, and whether it "works" or not is the real test.)

I cited in an earlier chapter the following rule of thumb on quotes: If the source has said something better than you can say it, quote the source. Otherwise, make the point in your own words. After all, you are the professional writer, not your source. (This is over and above the notion that we quote people to convey personality and emotion, and it is no contradiction. If the source's own words convey his or her personality or feelings better than you can describe them, then you still have the green light to indulge in quoting the source.)

Here's a fictionalized example of an unnecessary quote. Let's say you're doing a story on a hurricane survivor in the South Carolina low country. You might write something like this:

Winds were so high that light poles bent or snapped in two, and plate glass windows in ocean front hotels were shattered. Cars were tossed from a parking lot and stacked on top of each other like junk yard wrecks. Highways leading out of town were clogged with disappointed tourists forced to cut short their vacations.

I think the above lead is adequate, if not quite brilliant. It's not as good as the Von Drehle selection on Hurrican Hugo I included in the chapter on observation, but let's agree that it is adequate.

But, you might have been tempted to quote an eyewitness instead. Employing an eyewitness report sounds good, doesn't it?

"I never saw winds like that before," said Joe Smith, who operates a coffee shop near the ocean front. "I was never more afraid in my life."

Quotes like the above are a dime a dozen. They're the antithesis of the "show, don't tell" model we really want for good, vivid journalistic writing. In the sample paragraph that preceded the quote, which could have been gleaned from several sources, we have at least an adequate picture of what things were like under the veil of the storm. Quoting just one person who had nothing interesting to say implies the reporter didn't do much reporting to begin with (otherwise he or she would have come up with a better quote), and it's really an unnecessary tying of the reporter's hands. The reporter is free to interview many people to glean the active, graphic details that make up a word-picture, and then put things in his or her own words. Quoting too often or carelessly defeats this.

I often like to think of quotes as punctuating a paragraph or section in a story. You'll see lots of well-written leads with only one quote in them—the very last paragraph in the lead, which then will be followed by the nut graf and/or the main body of the story.

> On Sunday, March 23, at 3:10 a.m., Hazel Cox, who was 90, died in her sleep in the Lockefield Village nursing home, a public facility for poor, sick people with no place else to go.
>
> She died clutching pale-blue rosary beads, her only possession other than a blond Barbie doll with a princess dress.
>
> Since Hazel Cox had no relatives, friends or money, a "removal service" took her tiny, crippled body to the Flanner & Buchanan Mortuary on High School Road for a pauper's burial.
>
> The next day the mortuary placed a death notice in the paper: "Hazel E. Cox, 90, anyone knowing a living relative, please contact Flanner and Bucahnan Mortuary, (555–7020)."
>
> No one did.
>
> "We get very few like this who are just nobody," mortuary manager Tim Taylor said.(Shaw, 1997b)

This is another lead by Bill Shaw, and it's very good. It describes action with just enough detail (the rosary, the Barbie doll) that you get the picture. It doesn't waste (or mince) words; you see how sad this woman's life was at her end without any need of maudlin writing or, as I like to say, without the writer pouring on the gravy too thick.

But the point here is how nicely the anecdote leads into the quote, or quotes, if you include the newspaper ad. The writer doesn't merely tell us the world put no value on the woman's life at her end; instead we learn this fact from the uncompromising, unsentimental quote at the end of the anecdotal lead.

Finally, one often can end the feature with a strong quote. The quote can be like the cherry on top of the dessert or the ribbon around a nicely wrapped gift package. A good quote is the finishing touch to many pieces.

Here's how Sharon Aschen's "affirmation of life" story ended:

> "It was a high," said Aschen. "I'm glad I did that. And if I'm lucky enough to live to my 50th birthday, which is Mother's Day, I'm going to do it again." (p. J02)

You wouldn't think there could be a hopeful ending to a story about dying of spinal cancer, but there it is.

Look back at the many full-text stories in this collection—most end with a quote.

13

Copyediting for Features

A former English professor by the name of Don Fry long was a writing coach at the Poynter Institute in Florida. Part of his job would take him to newsrooms around the country teaching journalists how to be better writers and copy editors (Fry, personal communication, 1995).

One of the cardinal sins any copy editor makes, he says, is to edit a story "from the bottom," which is a way of noting that some copy editors simply cut a story's ending when it is too long to fill the allotted space.

Fry tells the story of sitting next to a copy editor in a major newspaper's newsroom and asking him if he ever did that—cut a story from the bottom without regard to its content or importance to the story? They talked for a few minutes about the evils of this practice and the copy editor said he never does it. Yet in the time Fry talked to him, and sat right next to him, the copy editor was "defining" the ends of several stories on his computer screen and deleting (cutting) them!

That practice is never excusable. Copy editors shouldn't do any editing to any story until they've read the story through. But cutting from the bottom is particularly egregious. Features are written with an ending, just like a good short story. You cannot cut a good feature story from the end any more than you can cut a punch line from a joke, or the exciting climax from a suspense novel.

One of the things many of you learned in a basic copyediting class is to cut, cut, and cut some more; to use shorter, simpler words instead of more complex language, regardless of nuance, subtlety, or complexity of language; to save inches at all costs. This is bad advice in the face of a well-written feature.

There's a related problem on the copy desk, and line editors sometimes suffer from this syndrome as well: They want to move important facts way up in the story; they want to turn the first part of a story into some kind of index or table of contents for the story to come; they cannot and will not wait for a story to unfold. Many of you will see in all this that the hated inverted pyramid is rearing its ugly head again. I fear that copy editors (and some reporters, admittedly) learned a little about the importance of the inverted pyramid when they studied journalism in college, and then never learned another thing about it in their lives.

This is all very wrong-headed thinking when it comes to well-written feature stories. For a copy editor to start trashing a feature story that has likely been written by one of the better writers in the paper, or which represents the more important work of a beat reporter, and which has almost certainly been read and edited by two or more line editors, is like a corporal in the army overriding instructions from a captain which already have been approved by even more senior officers. You better have some very good reasons to start changing things.

It's a perennial battle in newsrooms: Who has more power, copy editors or reporters? This is one of the most destructive aspects of life in the newsroom, too. With regard to features, the proper role of the copy editor is to challenge only clear misuses of the language and/or AP style (but not writing style), challenge the reporting (what's been left out that should be included? what questions just haven't been answered? what misstatements of fact are about to get into print?), and fix real errors in grammar and syntax.

If a story must be shortened—and that happens—then the copy editor should try to consult with the writer. If that's not possible, the surgery must be done with a view to preserving as much of the wholeness of the story as possible. That means picking and plucking paragraphs throughout the story, but not cutting from the bottom wantonly. I would fire any copy editor who routinely cut stories from the bottom.

Copy editors often say the story must be made understandable to the average reader; copy editors think it is their job to dumb down stories, in other words. I once interviewed a top editor at World Book Encyclopedia and asked about the rumor that all World Book articles were written very simply in the beginning, then in a more complex way near the end.

"Not true," the editor protested, although he had heard that misconception before. World Book articles always are written in the language most appropriate for the type of person expected to look up the article, he explained. This meant that an entry on Einstein's theory of relativity, which might be read by a physics student in high school or even college, is not going to be made overly simple; it meant that an article on butterflies probably would be written for (and read by) a school kid doing a report in third grade.

And so it goes with features (and all newspaper writing, frankly.) *All stories should be written and edited at a level appropriate for the person most likely to read the story.* This terrible notion that there is an average reader out there who spends "only 18 ½ minutes" with the paper each day is ruining good writing in our papers. There is no more such a thing as the average reader than there is the average American family with 1⅔ children. Frankly, I'd like to see what "two-thirds" of a child looks like, anyway. These are all statistical averages and means and norms and should never be taken at face value.

Some readers will spend all their time with one or two good stories in the paper each day; other readers just scan the headlines and pictures. From such people we come up with an average, but there is no such thing as average! I mention all this because, in my long years of experience, it is the copy desk that is most insistent we have to write for the average reader. Get this notion of average out of your head if you want to be a good copy editor on the features desk.

14

Using Databases

More research is expected of reporters today, in part because of the easy access to online databases. Whether you're in Waco, Texas, or Walla Walla, Washington, there is no excuse for being uninformed on almost any topic you may be writing about.

It helps if you have a personal computer at home with access to the Internet, but this is by no means a prerequisite to doing good research. First, most college libraries provide better access than the commercial Internet service providers, so you'll probably be doing your background research at the library anyway. (Many college libraries allow you to access their online services and databases remotely, i.e., from your home or dorm.)

But even municipal and public libraries now typically provide Internet access on computers you can use on their premises, and they always offer training classes on a regular basis. You may be restricted to a certain number of minutes for any particular session, and you may find it worthwhile to come at the least busy times of day (Georgia Southern University library staff always advised students to come to Henderson Library between 4 am and 6 am for the easiest, fastest connections, and they were right).

And, even if you still don't want to use computers at all, there are plenty of other easy-to-use research tools available to you at virtually any college or public library.

Now, imagine you have been assigned to do a story on breast cancer. It's a big topic, and there are a host of stories you can do. The only thing I would stress is that you are not doing a research paper; you are doing background reading for an article for a journalism class, school newspaper, or you are freelancing an article to a breast cancer newsletter or the local newspaper. You will include some of your research in your article just so you can educate the public, but mostly you're doing the research so you'll be a better-informed writer.

Perhaps the news peg or spur for your story is the Race for the Cure, a breast cancer fund-raiser, or it's breast cancer awareness month. Perhaps a prominent local person has just revealed she has breast cancer, or the local hospital or university has announced a breakthrough in breast cancer research or treatment. Something like this almost certainly will be your news peg.

Let's say you are doing a story in connection with breast cancer awareness month (or week, as the case may be). Let's say furthermore that you really don't know much about breast cancer: To borrow a phrase from the late American humorist Will Rogers, "I only know what I read in the newspapers," and that often isn't much.

I show you three different tacks in this chapter that you can follow to do research on your topic without registering for a special science class; two of the tacks are guaranteed to provide you with breast cancer patients and/or survivors who will talk about their personal experiences with the disease and treatment. It is these personal interviews that will distinguish your article from a mere research paper.

Search Engines

It'll be helpful if you follow along at an actual computer terminal.

My favorite search engine is Lycos, but you could use Web Crawler, Yahoo, Infoseek, or any of several others. Search engines are those features of computers that let you do keyword searches once you are online. Typically, your computer screen will have a prompt (I think of it as a button or tab) marked "search"; click on it and any of several search engines will appear. Some newer screens will actually display the search feature in the name of one of the proprietary search engines. For example, the home page at *The Indianapolis Star* always offers Infoseek.

For my search I simply choose the keywords "breast cancer" and search only the "TOP 5%" sites as calculated by Lycos. Search engines typically give you way too many "hits" when you are searching a topic, so limiting yourself to the top sites effectively narrows the mass of material you may have to wade through. (It may also cause you to miss some interesting, but relatively obscure alternative source, of course.)

On the Lycos screen, I click on the "Go for it" prompt.

Lycos immediately gives me a choice of organizations and web sites that seem promising; I select the "National Alliance of Breast Cancer Organizations." Within their home page I have a number of further choices; I click on "National Support Groups" because I anticipate needing to speak with actual patients and/or survivors in my area.

This immediately brings me to a page titled, "How to Find a Breast Cancer Support Group." I am prompted to click on the line "H-M" because I live in Indiana, but you would click on the appropriate line for the state you live in. You then would be taken to addresses for actual organizations in your area for follow-up.

This page provides me with a toll-free phone number for the American Cancer Society, as well as the organization Y-ME (a cancer support group for victims), either of which would have put me in touch with real cancer patients and/or survivors.

Going back to the original "breast cancer" keyword search on Lycos, remember that there were many other home pages Lycos offered me at the time. Some would have been more technical than others; all had brief summaries of breast cancer prevalence in the United States and other useful statistics.

The point is that within minutes I have been able to print out some fact sheets on breast cancer; I have found web sites and/or phone numbers for further research; and I have the potential to talk to real people for my story.

Lexis-Nexis

For years this database was the exclusive domain of corporate executives, high-powered attorneys, and research institutions willing to pay the hefty per-minute price tag to search this incredibly rich database. Beginning in 1998, however, the owners of Lexis-Nexis opened a web site on the Internet they call Lexis-Nexis Universe. I still prefer the older, Windows-based Lexis-Nexis database that I can access from a dedicated terminal at Indiana University, but Lexis-Nexis promises that, in time, their "Universe" will provide access to most anything in their database that journalists and students might really want.

For some reason, some people have trouble using Lexis-Nexis, especially in the Windows version. I think it is the expression "boolean searches" that frightens people. In fact, you do carry out "boolean searches" on Lexis-Nexis, but I assure you this has nothing to do with *Star Trek: Deep Space Nine*, or anything of the kind. For our purposes, "boolean searches" simply refer to connecting words, especially "and." This allows you to search for online articles that contain all of the keywords you designate, and only such articles. For example, I could search "breast and cancer and fatality and United States and 1995" to get breast cancer fatality data for 1995 in the United States.

Typically, you'll click on a Lexis-Nexis or Nexis screen (Nexis is the news database of the service; Lexis is the legal database and may be excluded from some libraries), and you may be asked to identify yourself by name and/or to identify your research.

All prompts are on-screen, so you really can't go wrong. The "Universe" version is similar to search engines in general: You identify a keyword, then search for it. If you're using the windows version, you'll see a double row menu bar at the top of the screen, with icons (small graphics or pictures) representing your different options. For example, a simple drawing of a handheld magnifying glass represents a "search." Other symbols represent the "library" you want to search (this is important in order to narrow your search somewhat). Then there are symbols for a "KWIC" or "FULL" text reading of the documents found, and so on. Most college and library subscribers to Lexis-Nexis do not let you print the full document with one click (this is an extra-cost option they don't want to pay for), so you almost always will have to click on the "print screen" option, one screen at a time, to print your full document. Of course, there's usually a download option onto your own diskette, but I always like a hardcopy of what I'm reading.

Now, let's say we're still doing that breast cancer story. On-screen prompts offer me various libraries; in a dry run at Indiana University's library I select GENMED for the following keywords "breast and cancer and fatality and United States and 1995" and get 20 documents. These all are from technical and medical journals; most seem too technical for me!

But the on-screen menu bar (again, this is the windows version I'm describing in detail) always offers the opportunity to "change library," which I do by clicking on the appropriate icon. I go into NEWS, and further limit my search to MAJPAP, which is "major papers." Think of all these libraries as reading rooms or collections in your favorite library; in a sense, Lexis-Nexis is simply a virtual library.

Lexis-Nexis saves my search terms for me and gives me another 20 or so hits from major papers. The articles are listed chronologically from most recent to oldest, which is useful; keywords I select always are highlighted in the text so I can scroll down the texts quickly.

I find lots of interesting information about breast cancer: It's the leading killer of women between 15 and 45, for example.

Lexis-Nexis also is superb in allowing users to modify the search, or start a new search; again, the on-screen menu bar shows you these options, and you just click on the appropriate icon, then type in your new search terms.

I did a story several years ago on a woman who introduced herself this way: "Hi, I'm a breast cancer diagnosis." In the course of the interview she talked about terrible swelling in her arm from chemotherapy, and how the doctors told her that it was "normal," that she'd have to "learn to live with it." There was a specific name to the condition, but I forgot what it was.

I did a new search on Lexis-Nexis, typing in "breast cancer and treatment and swelling" as my search terms (same as keywords, really). About 220 articles popped up this time; the very first had the word I was really looking for, namely "lymphedema." This condition is worth a major Sunday feature by itself.

And so it goes. This example should give you an idea of how easy it is to look up information on breast cancer, or any topic, on Lexis-Nexis, and just how flexible and powerful the database is for giving you additional information you didn't even know you were looking for.

Encyclopedia of Associations

This is an old standby. You can find the *Encyclopedia of Associations* online now, but I'll limit this discussion to the bound volumes any library should have. The *Encyclopedia of Associations* is a three-volume set, with a keyword index comprising Volume 3. Look up a key word—cancer, or breast cancer—and you will be given a numerical reference to either Volume 1 or Volume 2 for associations and organizations related to this topic.

For example, under "breast cancer," I find the National Alliance of Breast Cancer Associations, which is entry 12371 in the encyclopedia. An address, executive officer, regular and toll-free phone and fax number, and e-mail address are included, as well as a brief description of the organization. "Serves as a resource for individuals seeking information about research, developments, and treatment options for breast cancer," the entry says at one point.

I'd call them if I were working on an appropriate story.

Under the word "cancer," I find dozens of entries, mostly clustered around the 12000 entry number (this is a bit like a Dewey Decimal system in the public library; once you find one title in the card catalog or electronic catalog, you know similar titles will be shelved nearby when you go to the stacks). A quick tour through some of these listings would have found additional suitable sources to contact for expert information, background information, and people to interview. My students have always had good luck working the *Encyclopedia of Associations*; most groups listed here want to communicate with you, and they will talk to students.

Typically, only national organizations are listed, but call the listed phone number and you'll be referred to local chapters (if any exist) for the topic you're researching. This is extremely important if you're looking for ordinary people to interview, not just experts. Many associations listed in this reference also publish helpful brochures and pamphlets.

The only caveat I'd issue is that they are typically advocacy groups with a certain point of view or agenda, that may or may not be conducive to an objective, fair-minded story. The way to deal with this potential problem, of course, is to talk to competing and alternative advocacy groups.

I once used the *Encyclopedia of Associations* to access a group called Parents of Murdered Children; I began with "children" in the keyword index. The group was based in Cincinnati, but had a chapter in a south Indianapolis suburb run by a UPS truck driver and his wife. Their teenage son had been murdered a couple of years earlier, less than a mile from home; the crime remained unsolved. The national chapter passed on my name to the local couple and they agreed to an interview.

There are countless other ways in which to use databases, and numerous databases and reference books we often ignore. My hometown newspaper in Bloomington, Indiana, did a computer search of courthouse records looking for any criminal charges filed against candidates in an upcoming sheriff's elections. The paper found two, including a case of domestic dispute against one of the leading candidates. The sheriff's candidate had completed a deferral program and so the charges were dismissed, but how embarrassing in any case! And, just think how easy it must have been to search computerized court records (which are, of course, public records that anyone can access) compared to doing an old-fashioned, time-consuming paper search.

My son loves to read the "Information Please Almanac," which is published annually and is available at any good bookstore. It's similar to the annual almanacs many top newspapers publish under their own names. There's a wealth of well-organized data in these collections on subjects ranging from old presidential elections to statistics about other nations of the world to geography to important dates and events in history to sports trivia. There's plenty of data on cancer and breast cancer in the one I'm looking at right now, too.

There also are countless web sites or home pages you may want to mark as "favorites" on your computer, or to "bookmark" for quick access in the future. If your first job takes you to the police beat (a common fate of beginning journalists), you'll find various online sources of crime and justice statistics you may want to bookmark and use, in addition to doing the usual "who, what, when, where, and how" overnight murder story.

Many colleges offer a library research methods course (or something similarly titled). Such a course, usually offered for one- or two-credit hours, should be invaluable. Register for it. As a reporter I know I'm spoiled by calling our reference librarians, but the more you can do on your own the better.

15

Breaking Into Newspapering

I remember when I first began stringing (working part-time or on occasional assignments) for the *St. Louis Globe-Democrat*. It was 1983 and I was teaching at the time in the school of journalism at Southern Illinois University-Carbondale, which is about two hours east and south of St. Louis. *The Globe-Democrat* had just closed its Southern Illinois bureau, which had been based in Carbondale, and the newspaper sent out flyers encouraging student journalists to cover stories for it. I announced this opportunity to students in several of my classes, but couldn't interest anyone.

So I began stringing for the St. Louis paper myself.

My first story was a feature on a wizened, old watchmaker who rented space in the small, creaky old railroad terminal in Carbondale. He was the only tenant; the trains all stopped at a new depot on the edge of town. Another story dealt with the week-long visit of a famous novelist to campus. I had loaned the man my three-speed upright bicycle to get around on, and included a description of him pedaling across the campus in my story.

In time, the *St. Louis Globe-Democrat* had a full-time opening for a feature writer, and I jumped ship. Moving from stringer, or correspondent or part-time status, to full-time staffer at a daily newspaper may not be common, but it happens.

The last time I checked, there were about 54,700 journalists working full time at the United States' approximately 1,600 daily newspapers (1998 Annual Survey by the American Society of Newspaper Editors). In truth, most earned their spot the old fashioned way: They were journalism school grads or majors who went straight from an undergraduate career to a newspaper job.

Those of you who are still in school should consult with your placement adviser; you should go to job fairs (and minorities should take advantage of minority job fairs); and everyone should be looking for internships, after your second year in school, if possible, but certainly after your third year. Sometimes you can create your own internship, even if it's just over winter break. I've known several students over the years who volunteered to work for their hometown newspapers while on winter break, which is a time when a lot of staffers like to take their vacations.

Realistically, the internship is your first job in the business. Most large journalism schools or departments will have a director or coordinator of internships. The most highly prized internships usually accept applications in the fall for the following summer.

Here are several web sites and addresses for internships and/or entry level jobs. The addresses and numbers were correct as of late 1997.

- The Dow Jones Newspaper Fund (DJNF) publishes "The Journalist's Road to Success" and "Newspapers, Diversity & You: A Career Guide," both available by writing DJNF, P.O. Box 300, Princeton, NJ 08543-0300, or by calling (609) 452–2820.
- The Society of Professional Journalists (SPJ) publishes a weekly newsletter typically listing more than 400 job openings, including about 100 fresh ones each week. Call (765) 653–3333, or write SPJ, P.O. Box 77, Greencastle, IN 46135.
- The Pulliam Fellowships. Ten spots are reserved each summer for graduating seniors at *The Indianapolis Star* and *News*, and at *The Arizona Republic*, which are all owned by the same company. You'll have a personal writing coach, guest lecturers, and many real assignments to help you build a great clip file, as well as support in looking for a permanent, full-time position once summer ends. The fellowship pays as much as most entry-level positions at other papers. Write to: The Pulliam Fellowships, c/o Indianapolis Newspapers Inc., 307 N. Pennsylvania St., Indianapolis IN 46204.
- A nice web site that contains a jobs board is www.reporters.net.

There are many others, the proverbial "too many to list." *Editor & Publisher* magazine, available at most libraries and by subscription, lists dozens of job openings weekly. Long Island (New York) *Newsday* newspaper holds regular minority job fairs. SPJ typically has workshops on landing that first job at many of its regional and annual meetings.

In preparing this chapter I spoke with several seasoned journalists for their views on the best way to break into the lineup, as it were, and for stories of how they got started in their careers.

"I always tell the same story, which is the importance of getting an internship," said Dennis Royalty (personal communication, May 1998), a bureau chief for *The Indianapolis Star* and *Indianapolis News*. "I'm always surprised by journalism students who don't try out for internships or don't write stories independently of class. That to me says they don't have the real love of journalism they'll need to succeed."

Royalty's first internship was with *The Star*, circa 1970. "I took advantage of it," he recalled. "I couldn't stay long enough. I took every assignment thrown at me."

That was between his junior and senior years at Indiana University. Later, he took a sportswriter's position at the now-defunct Bloomington *Courier-Tribune* and covered basketball coach Bob Knight's first season. Royalty's career in Bloomington died, however, when the newspaper folded in 1973.

"I was lucky enough to know within the next three or four days that I had another job," he said. "I still attribute it to that internship I had."

Yes—the happy ending here was predictable: Royalty was hired at *The Star*, by the same editor he had interned for 2 years earlier. Nevertheless, there are exceptions to every rule, and every year people who did not major in journalism in college, or who worked in other fields after college, get newspaper jobs. I'm one case in point, as noted above. I decided to call the guy who hired me for my first full-time newspaper job in St. Louis in 1984.

Patrick Gauen, a former managing editor of the *St. Louis Globe-Democrat*, now is Illinois political correspondent for the *St. Louis Post-Dispatch*.

"Most of the people I work with did go to 'j school' or started working for newspapers right out of college," Gauen (personal communication, May 1998) told me. "But one of the better people I worked with was Bill Anderson, who had a master's in zoology and worked in that field for several years."

Midcareer, Anderson earned a bachelor's degree at SIU-Evansville and worked part-time for smaller papers, then got on full-time at the *Globe-Democrat*. Alas, that paper is now defunct, but Anderson continues to work in public relations.

Gauen remembered another ex-*Globe* staffer who was an insurance salesman. The man had done some "stringing" for a few newspapers, that is, writing occasional news stories on a correspondent or freelance basis, and Gauen hired him.

Gauen himself is an exception to the rule. A college dropout who once thought of being an architect, his first newspaper job was for his hometown paper in Collinsville, Illinois. He's had a fine career without the degree; he even teaches journalism courses at St. Louis' prestigious Washington University.

Another interesting exception to the rule is someone you met earlier in this book. Marie C. Franklin, author of the trend story on business professionals who, midcareer, become teachers, is herself a former school teacher who became an education writer for the *Boston Globe*. She started her career at a smaller paper, writing for a weekly in Brookline, Massachusetts, shortly after the birth of her first baby, and after teaching for 11 years.

For 1½ years she covered municipal council hearings, board meetings, and all kinds of government business, often carrying her daughter with her in a little papoose.

Not surprisingly, one of her first feature sales to the *Boston Globe* was on signing and keeping babysitters.

"I was 33 when I was hired as an (education) editor" at the *Globe*, Franklin (personal communication, May 1998) recalled. "That was a little later in life. I was concerned there might be a prejudice against me because I had not been in journalism all the time."

Since 1986 Franklin has had what is essentially a permanent part-time position at *The Globe*, which has allowed her to raise her two daughters while pursuing a career. She began by contributing occasional stories to a children's section.

"An editor said, 'If you've got some talent and some drive you'll get noticed.' I thought, 'That's right.'"

Franklin regularly contributes education stories to the paper, and says her teaching background has been invaluable in her beat. "Absolutely," she declared. "Teachers feel I understand their profession, their challenges, and their joys because I had been in the profession myself."

16

Spell Checkers

Many people think that spelling is no longer important; the spell checker will catch any mistakes. Never has anything been as badly named as the spell checker, though. Spell checkers are nothing but small databases that match your words with words in the database: If there's a match, it's assumed you've spelled the word correctly. If there's no match, then you may have misspelled a word.

Suppose you've used the wrong word, but spelled it correctly, though? The classic example is to use the word "there," which refers to location, in lieu of "their," which refers to possession, or vice versa. Older spell checkers have no idea which word you intended (admittedly, some modern grammar checkers would catch this mistake).

Spell checkers also annoyingly will stop at many proper nouns or names of persons, although the better ones let you add words to the database.

The following is a letter to the editor that ran on p. A9 in the November 24, 1997, *Indianapolis Star* that illustrates all that is wrong with spell checkers. (© *The Indianapolis Star*, reprinted with permission.)

> Too the teacher an the student who thought that bean able to spell wasp knot necessary, because of "Spellcheck," this entire parachute was composted an verified one my computer, and ewe can sea the results—gibberish.
>
> Hour local newspaper in Hamilton County a parent lee uses "Spellcheck" for there headlines, suck as: "Supermarket robbers still on lamb" and "Police seize 100 viles."
>
> Wise up, people, you can't deep end on machines two dew everything. Sum times wee knead too use hour gray mutter.
>
> —Ken Casper
> Noblesville, IN.

REFERENCES

Aamidor, A. (1987, December 10). Cosmetic surgery. *The Indianapolis News*, p. C1.

Aamidor, A. (1989, March 28). Surviving a century. *The Indianapolis News*, p. D1.

Aamidor, A. (1992, January 10). Storefront Politics. *The Indianapolis News*, pp. B1–B2.

Aamidor, A. (1994, July 31). Nascarnival. *The Indianapolis Star*, pp. J1–J2.

Aamidor, A. (1995, October 9). Upward Mobility. *The Indianapolis Star*, pp. D1–D2.

Aamidor, A. (1996, April 7). Russian to the altar: American men extend hands across the sea, seeking hands in marriage. *The Indianapolis Star*, pp. J1–J2.

Aamidor, A. (1997, August 10). Hittin' the highway. *The Indianapolis Star*, p. J1.

Aamidor, A. (1998a, January. 9). History mystery. *The Indianapolis Star*, pp. D1–D2.

Aamidor, A. (1998b, March 22). Party of her life. *The Indianapolis Star*, p. J1.

American Society of Newspaper Editors. (1998). Annual Survey: Author.

Balough, M. (1996, January/February.) Changing techniques: Austin experiment may alter the way journalists measure populace's mood; deliberative polling of presidential aspirants in Texas. *The Quill, 84*(1), pp. 20–22.

Berkow, I. (1996, March 31). At Robinson's side, Reese helped change baseball. *The New York Times*, p. 1.

Blundell, W. (1988). *The art and craft of feature writing.* New York: Plume/Penguin.

Bosworth Jr., C. (1997, September 1). Fading Beauty: JonBenet Ramsey case blamed for decline in pageant entries. *St. Louis Globe-Democrat*, p. 4B.

Burck, J. (1997, August 25). Drivers reminded to stop for school buses. *The (Bloomington, Indiana) Herald-Times*, pp. 1–2.

Camp, J. (1985, May 12). Life on the land: An American Farm Family. *St. Paul Pioneer Press*, p. A1.

Casper, K. (1997, November 24). Spellchecked. Letters. *The Indianapolis Star*, p. A9.

Dorschner, J. (1991, October 27). Stayin' alive: Ed Van Houten and America's health-care dilemma. Reprinted in the *Chicago Tribune Magazine*, pp. 14–20.

Dumanoski, D. (1990, March 5). Rethinking man's place: One earth. *The Boston Globe*, p. 27.

Dunn, M. (1998, January 25). Endeavour hooks up with Mir, and Wolf does flips. *The Buffalo News*, p. 2A.

Franklin, J. (1994). *Writing for story.* New York: Plume/Penguin.

Franklin, M. C. (1997, January 12). The lure of the classroom. *The Boston Globe*, p. F1.

Gillaspy, J. (1997, July 5). High-speed chase ends in death. *The Indianapolis Star*, p. B2.

Hagen, P. (1997, January 22). Child pageants debated after 6-year-old's death. *The Indianapolis Star*, p. B1.

Harker, J. (1994, October 25). Slavery: Nations built on slavery; slavery took a huge social and economic toll on its victims. Now some people want this historic debt repaid. *The Guardian* (London), p. 11.

Higgins, A. (1998, June 27). AIDS report. *The Indianapolis Star*, p. A11.

Jensen, E. (1997, October 14). Wine gets a makeover: A complex Zinfandel becomes a power 'zin'. *The Wall Street Journal*, p. 1A, column 6.

Kelley, T. (1997, April 28). Murder.on.the.net: The killing of JonBenet Ramsey has become an online obsession. *Baltimore Sun*, p. 1D.

Kiefer, M. (1996, October 3). A quiet voice against the death penalty: Amnesty International's Dr. Daniel Georges-Abeyie cooly argues the case against the punishment in our hang-'em high state. *Phoenix New Times*, Features, p. 1.

Landsberg, M. (1998, January 26). Dying young—a way of life in gloomy Russia. Associated Press feature appeared in *The Chicago Tribune*, p. 8.

Leo, J. (1997, December. 1). Enola, we hardly knew ye. *U.S. News and World Report*, p. 16.

Miller, M. (1994, July 20). Fat pharm. *The Wall Street Journal*, p. 1A, column 6.

Mitchell, A. (1998, January 23). Both sides rally to mark abortion ruling. *The New York Times*, p. A19.

Moore, G. E. (1903). *Principia Ethica*. Cambridge, England: Cambridge University Press.

O'Hanlon, A. (1997, March 16). A trend gives cause to blush: Use of makeup among young girls. *The Washington Post, Wall Street Journal*, p. A1.

Patterson, G. A. (1992, March 10). Tough business. Tough Business. *Wall Street Journal*, p. A1.

Rakowsky, J., & MacQuarrie, B. (1997, August 25). More grief comes to a grief-stricken region. Originally appeared in *The Boston Globe*, p. 1.

Schmitt, B. (1997, August 11). City's escort services: It's just companionship. *Savannah Morning News*, pp. C1– C2.

Selz, M. (1995, November 15). Old style journalism for today's turned-off reader. *The Wall Street Journal*, p. B1, column 3.

Shaw, B. (1997a, April 4). Spanning past and future: Amish-raised Amos B. Schwartz rebuilds treasures of the past. *The Indianapolis Star*, pp. B1–B2.

Shaw, B. (1997b, April 14). A prayer for Mrs. Cox. *The Indianapolis Star*, p. E1.

Shaw, B. (1998, March 15). When faced with heartache 101-year-old Ann Vollmer has put on a brave face and gotten on with life by painting the green fence. *The Indianapolis Star*, p. J1.

Staff report. (1997, August 13). 377 died last year in chases. *The Indianapolis Star*, p. A2.

Thompson, C. (1998, January 2). Psychics strike out: No predictions for '97 came true. *The Ottawa Citizen*, p. A10.

Thompson, H. S. (1967, May 14). The "Hashbury" is the capital of the hippies. *The New York Times Magazine, 29*, pp. 120–124.

Unsigned editorial. (1997, July 12). Perils of the chase. *The Indianapolis Star*. p. A10.

von Drehle, D. (1989, September 23). Shaken survivors witness pure fury. *The Miami Herald*, p. 1.

Wessel, K. (1996, December 13). Bystanders, police often hurt: Dangerous chases spur police to look at policies and options. *The Courier-Journal*, pp. 1A–2A.

Author Index

Subject Index

S

T

V

W